Chinese

The Chinese Language Learning Guide for Beginners

© Copyright 2020

All Rights Reserved. No part of this book may be reproduced in any form without permission in writing from the author. Reviewers may quote brief passages in reviews.

Disclaimer: No part of this publication may be reproduced or transmitted in any form or by any means, mechanical or electronic, including photocopying or recording, or by any information storage and retrieval system, or transmitted by email without permission in writing from the publisher.

While all attempts have been made to verify the information provided in this publication, neither the author nor the publisher assumes any responsibility for errors, omissions or contrary interpretations of the subject matter herein.

This book is for entertainment purposes only. The views expressed are those of the author alone, and should not be taken as expert instruction or commands. The reader is responsible for his or her own actions.

Adherence to all applicable laws and regulations, including international, federal, state and local laws governing professional licensing, business practices, advertising and all other aspects of doing business in the US, Canada, UK or any other jurisdiction is the sole responsibility of the purchaser or reader.

Neither the author nor the publisher assumes any responsibility or liability whatsoever on the behalf of the purchaser or reader of these materials. Any perceived slight of any individual or organization is purely unintentional.

Contents

PART 1: CHINESE FOR BEGINNERS 1
INTRODUCTION 2
SECTION 1: THE VERY BASICS 5
CHAPTER 1: THE CHINESE ALPHABET 6
CHAPTER 2: NOUNS, PRONOUNS, AND ADJECTIVES 13
CHAPTER 3: VERBS AND AUXILIARY VERBS 20
CHAPTER 4: NUMERALS AND MEASURE WORDS 26
CHAPTER 5: AUXILIARY WORDS 33
SECTION 2: GRAMMAR 39
CHAPTER 6: PHRASES AND SENTENCE ELEMENTS 40
CHAPTER 7: SIMPLE AND COMPLEX SENTENCES 49
SECTION 3: CONVERSATION 54
CHAPTER 8: BASIC GREETINGS 56
CHAPTER 9: INTRODUCING YOURSELF 59
CHAPTER 10: FORMULATING QUESTIONS AND DIALOGUE: 68
APPENDIX: VOCABULARY 87
GLOSSARY OF NOUNS 87

PART 2: MASTERING CHINESE WORDS 115
INTRODUCTION 116
SECTION 1 118
1,200 BASIC WORDS 118
CHAPTER 1. NOUNS 119
CHAPTER 2. VERBS AND AUXILIARY VERBS 139
CHAPTER 3. PRONOUNS AND ADJECTIVES 160
CHAPTER 4. NUMERALS AND MEASURE WORDS 171
CHAPTER 5. ADVERBS, PREPOSITIONS, AND CONJUNCTIONS 174
SECTION 2 180
LEARN 1,300 OTHER WORDS 180
CHAPTER 6. NOUNS (A ~ Q) 181
CHAPTER 7 NOUNS (R ~ Z) 195
CHAPTER 8. VERBS (A ~ L) 206
CHAPTER 9 VERBS (M ~ Z) 220
CHAPTER 10. OTHER CONTENT AND FUNCTION WORDS (A ~ L) 234
CONCLUSION 252

Part 1: Chinese for Beginners

A Comprehensive Guide for Learning the Chinese Language Quickly

INTRODUCTION

The Chinese language (or group of related languages) is spoken by the Han, who constitute 94% of China's population. One word for the language in Chinese is 汉语 (hàn yǔ). The Chinese language is divided into several major dialects (with many sub-dialects). Speakers of different dialects can in some cases find each other unintelligible, but are brought together by the fact that they share a common script. *Chinese for Beginners* describes the primary and official dialect, which is known by many names: Mandarin, Modern Standard Chinese, or *Putonghua* (common speech). This is a practical textbook designed for foreigners who are interested in learning Chinese through self-study and help them effectively master basic Chinese communication skulls within a short period of time.

In the last 20 years, more and more people from different parts of the world have come to China. Everybody experiences their own story and is often shocked by the changes in this fast-growing country. For expats living in China, many want and need to learn Mandarin Chinese. However, due to work commitments during the day and family activities after hours, it is sometimes difficult find the time to attend full-time language classes.

As professional language instructors with years of experience in corporate Chinese training, we have found that most language learning textbooks are designed for full-time training over a long term. It has been very difficult to find a practical book to help people start communicating as soon as possible. Therefore, we made up our mind and wrote the book *Chinese for Beginners* in 2020.

To make sure that the content is both practical and fun, we chose vocabulary based on the *HSK Guideline for Chinese Words and Characters*. We also used many words and dialogues that concern Chinese society as well as a foreigner's daily life, study, and work in China. In terms of grammar, we made explicit and practical examples to help users apply these points in a flexible manner. Language points are arranged from easiest to hardest and simplest forms to most complicated. Explanations present material in a way which meets the needs of students and is easy to learn.

Focusing on conversation, *Chinese for Beginners* was designed for those who can only read the book several times a week. The full book can be finished in a month. In order to help different types of readers find what they want to improve through this book, we have divided the book into four parts:

Part one begins with proper pronunciation in Mandarin. Readers using this book will get thorough training in phonetics. We introduce, explain, and emphasize points that are typical in Chinese phonetics and particularly difficult for beginners to grasp. Readers will learn numbers, months, and days of the week. After basic knowledge of articles, nouns, pronouns, prepositions, and adjectives is introduced.

Part two introduces basic Chinese grammar, including some special Chinese sentence structures which are very popular in daily oral Chinese. Since language is such an important aspect of Chinese culture, we also introduce elements of politeness to help learners to deal with common social situations.

Part three covers a wide range of typical situations in a students' daily social life including "Basic Greetings", "Introducing Yourself", "Buying and Ordering", "At Work", "At School/College", "Travelling", "Socializing", "Formal Events", and other common encounters. The language used is natural, standard, and vivid. Attention has been given to introducing aspects of Chinese culture while maintaining a level suitable for beginners. In these ways, the basic material is covered thoroughly while things are kept interesting.

Finally, we have an appendix to introduce you more nouns and verbs. All words are written in characters and phonetic transcriptions in the *pinyin* system with their speech portions and English equivalents provided. In order to provide students with a more exact understanding of the meanings and the usages of words. Some words are also accompanied with explanations rather than just English equivalents. Nevertheless, students should not expect to learn the meaning and usage of word by depending only on the English translation, which will often hold true only for a particular context.

Chinese for Beginners is also a good choice for people who would like to take an intensive course before going to China for business or pleasure.

Learning basic Chinese is not as difficult as you may think at first. Even the simplest knowledge of the language will enhance your experience. Our wish is to help you enjoy your life in China. We sincerely hope that learners may benefit from *Chinese for Beginners* and achieve more progress in the future. We firmly believe that more and more friends will come to China and start learning this ancient language. Good luck!

Section 1: THE VERY BASICS

Chapter 1: The Chinese Alphabet

Everybody knows that Chinese is a kind of pictographic language. Each word is made of characters. Each character is monosyllabic and has its own pronunciation. Chinese people mark the pronunciation of characters in pinyin (Chinese phonetic alphabets). There are two groups of alphabets in pinyin. One group is used at the beginning of a syllable and is called initials. The other group follows initials that are called finals.

There are 23 initials in modern Chinese:

b-, p-, m-, f-, d-, t-, n-, l-, g-, k-, h-, j-, q-, x-, z-, c-, s-, r-, zh-, ch-, sh-, y-, w-

The final with only one vowel is called a simple final. There are six of them:

-a, -o, -e, -i, -u, -ü

Finals made up of two or three vowels are called compound finals. There are 13 of them:

-ai, -ao, -ou, -ei, -ia, -ie, -iao, -ua, -uo, -uai, -üe, -iu, -ui

Finals with nasal endings are finals followed by –n or –ng. There are 16 of them:

-an, -ang, -ong, -en, -eng, -in, -ing, -ian, -iang, -iong, -eng, -un, -uan, -uang, -ün, -üan

Potential Trouble Spots

1. For a completed syllable, finals including i, u, or ü and finals starting with one of them should follow an initial. Finals that include a, o, or e and finals that start with one of them can be an independent syllable.

2. When -ü, -üe, -üan, and -ün follow j-, q-, x-, or y-, the two dots on the top of them are dropped. As such, it is yue and not yüe; yuan and not yüan. In addition, j-, q-, and x- can only combine with finals that start with -i and -ü.

3. The retroflex sounds: zh-, ch-, sh-, and r-. These initials are called retroflex sounds because they are all pronounced with the tongue curved back into the middle of mouth. For the first three of these, there is a corresponding sound that is pronounced further forward in the mouth, and one key to mastering standard Chinese pronunciation is being able to distinguish between the retroflex initial and its more forward counterpart. The pairs are:

zh- and j-. Both sound something like the "j" in "jump", but for zh-, the tip of the tongue is a little further back and for j- it is further forward.

ch- and q-. Both are like the "ch" in "chip", but for ch-, the tongue is further back and for q- it is further forward.

sh- and x-. Both are like the "sh" in "ship", but for sh-, the tongue is further back and for x-, it is further forward.

Retroflex sounds are more typical of northern Chinese speech than that of other parts of China; in fact, in many parts of China, people pronounce all these sounds with their tongue forward. zh- thus becomes z-, ch- becomes c-, and sh- becomes s-. While you should try to pronounce them in a standard manner, your ears need to get used to the many Chinese speakers who don't make these distinctions. You may also take comfort in the fact that many Chinese find the distinction between these pairs as troublesome as you may.

One way the sounds above are distinguished from each other is by the position of the tongue. They are also distinguished as much or more by the fact that j-, q-, and x- are always followed by a high front vowel, either –i or –ü, while zh-, ch-, and sh- never are. As such, even if you pronounce both members of a pair the same way, there is little probability of confusion as long as you get the rest of the word right.

4. In addition to the retroflex sounds discussed above, there are a few other sounds in Chinese that are just plain difficult for English speakers to make.

Chief amongst the trouble makers is the initial retroflex sound r-. It is pronounced like the "r" in "rank", but with the tongue just a bit higher so that is buzzes ever so slightly. Again, in many parts of China, people don't make this sound in a way that would pass for standard in Beijing, so you will be allowed some latitude in getting this one right.

The next one is c-. This "ts" sound does exist in English but is never present in the beginning of words. To make it, first say "cats" and then eliminate the "ca-" part.

English does not have the –ü sound. The simplest explanation is that it is a combination of "ooo" and "eee". To make it, make an "eee" sound with your jaw, and then round your lips for an "ooo" without moving your jaw.

5. On a whole, the *Pinyin* system is quite logical, though there are a few anomalies that may trip you up of you are not careful.

The -i. Usually this is pronounced like "ee" as in "he". But after the c-, s-, z-, ch-, sh-, zh-, or r-, it is pronounced as a short vowel, similar to the "i" in "it". The easiest way to cope with this is just to memorize that the following spellings require the short sound: ci, si, zi, zhi, chi, shi, and ri.

The -e. When alone, this is pronounced like "uh" in English, similar to the "u" in "under". In the following combinations, it is pronounced as follows:

The -ie sounds like the "ye" in "yes".

The -ue like the "we" in "wet".

The ye, again, sounds like the "ye" in "yes".

The -ian. Despite the "a", this sound is pronounced like the word "yen". Moreover, yan is also pronounced as "yen".

The -ui. This is pronounced like "way". We might expect this sound to be spelled as -uei, but no such luck. At least it isn't spelled "weigh".

Tones

Among the components of a Chinese syllable, there is also a tone besides the initial and the final. Altogether, there are four tones:

The first tone (the high tone)

The second tone (the rising tone)

The third tone (the falling-rising tone)

The fourth tone (the falling tone)

Syllables with same initials and finals in different tones usually have different meanings. For example:

tū, the Chinese character 秃, which means to be bold.

tú, the Chinese character 图, which means a map or a painting

tǔ, the Chinese character 土, which means earth or soil.

tù, the Chinese character 兔, which means a rabbit.

If a syllable preceded by another one is not stressed, it loses its tonal value and becomes short and weak. We call this the neutral tone, for example:

姐姐（jiě jie）older sister

孩子（hái zi）child

便宜（pián yi）cheap

In modern Chinese, there is a special grammatical phenomenon called tone-sandi.

When two 3rd tones are next to each other, the first one changes into a 2nd tone.

手表（shǒu biǎo）wrist watch

你好（nǐ hǎo）hello

很冷（hěn lěng）very cold

When 一 is placed before a syllable carrying the 4th tone, it is read in the 2nd tone (yí). When placed before a syllable carrying the 1st tone, the 2nd tone or the 3rd tone, it is read in the 4th tone (yì). When it is read independently or at the end of a word, 一 is pronounced as its original tone (yī).

"不" is pronounced in the 2nd tone (bú) when it precedes a 4th tone syllable. The tone of 不 does not change when it stands by itself or precedes a 1st, 2nd or a 3rd tone, pronounced (bù).

Exercise

1. Make a distinction between these difficult sounds:

b- and p-

辫子（biàn zi）pigtail

骗子（piàn zi）liar

d- and t-

读书（dú shū）reading

图书（tú shū）books

g- and k-

天宫（tiān gōng）heavenly palace

天空（tiān kōng）sky

zh- and ch-

竹子（zhú zi）bamboo

厨子（chú zi）cook

j- and q-

捐钱（juān qián）to denote

圈钱（quān qián）to collect money illegally

q- and x-

情形（qíng xíng）condition, situation, circumstances

行刑（xíng xíng）to execute

j- and x-

聚集（jù jí）to gather

续集（xù jí）sequel

s- and sh-

散开（sǎn kāi）to scatter

闪开（shǎn kāi）to get out of the way

c- and s-

一次（yí cì）one time

疑似（yí sì）seemingly certain but at the same time uncertain

z- and c-

没做（méi zuò）didn't do something

没错（méi cuò）didn't go wrong

-an and -en

瞻仰（zhān yǎng）to look at with reverence

真痒（zhēn yǎng）really itchy

-ang and -eng

东方（dōng fāng）east

东风（dōng fēng）east wind

-an and -ang

山口（shān kǒu）mountain pass

伤口（shāng kǒu）wound

-en and -eng

渗水（shèn shuǐ）to leak water

圣水（shèng shuǐ）holy water

2. Make a distinction between these different tones:

奴隶（nú lì）slave

努力（nǔ lì）to make great efforts

同班（tóng bān）classmate

同伴（tóng bàn）companion

仔细（zǐ xì）careful

自习（zì xí）self-study

松树（sōng shù）pine tree

松鼠（sōng shǔ）squirrel

徽章（huī zhāng）badge

会长（huì zhǎng）president of an association
孤立（gū lì）to isolate
鼓励（gǔ lì）to encourage
重视（zhòng shì）to attach importance to
忠实（zhōng shí）faithful
真鲜（zhēn xiān）really tasty
真咸（zhēn xián）really salty
真险（zhēn xiǎn）really dangerous
针线（zhēn xiàn）sewing
争执（zhēng zhí）dispute
整治（zhěng zhì）to fix or repair
正直（zhèng zhí）honest
政治（zhèng zhì）politics

3. Read the following words and pay attention to the neutral tones:

妈妈（mā ma）mother
回来（huí lai）to come back
办法（bàn fa）idea, method
东西（dōng xi）thing
棉花（mián hua）cotton
帽子（mào zi）hat, cap

4. Read the following words and pay attention to tone-sandhi

舞蹈（wǔ dǎo）dance
女友（nǚ yǒu）girlfriend
影响（yǐng xiǎng）influence
引导（yǐn dǎo）guidance
表演（biǎo yǎn）to act
野草（yě cǎo）weeds

Chapter 2: Nouns, Pronouns, and Adjectives

Nouns

A word denoting the name of a person or a thing is called a noun. Nouns in Chinese are not specifically identified as being nouns except in the case of those with suffixes such as 子 (zi), 儿 (er), 头 (tóu), etc. Generally, a noun can be preceded by a numeral and measure word combination but cannot be modified by adverbs.

Nouns can be assigned to different categories with reference to their grammatical properties. In general, we have common nouns, abstract nouns, and proper nouns.

Chinese nouns do not under any circumstances inflect for case, gender, or number. Therefore, in a language without definite or indefinite articles like Chinese, the reference of unmarked nouns is influenced by a number of factors: context, sentence type, the position of the noun in relation to the verb in the sentence, and the nature of the verb itself. When we use the noun 书 (shū) book, for instance, we have no way of determining whether it means "the book" or "books" in general until we place it in a sentence.

There are a group of nouns that have an inbuilt notion of plurality. For example:

父母（fù mǔ）parents
夫妻（fū qī）a married couple
子女（zǐ nǔ）children
师生（shī shēng）teachers and students
亲友（qīn yǒu）friends and relatives
财产（cái chǎn）possessions
树木（shù mù）trees
文具（wén jù）stationery
车辆（chē liàng）vehicles
花朵（huā duǒ）flowers
马匹（mǎ pǐ）horses
纸张（zhǐ zhāng）paper
砖块（zhuān kuài）bricks

Note that the last five examples above are formed by tagging measure words (辆、朵、匹、张、块) to nouns (车、花、马、纸、砖). If we put numerals and measure words in front of the nouns, they will still make sense.

一辆车（yí liàng chē）a car
两朵花（liǎng duǒ huā）two flowers
三匹马（sān pǐ mǎ）three horses
四张纸（sì zhāng zhǐ）four pieces of paper
五块砖（wǔ kuài zhuān）five bricks

The suffix 们 (men) can be added to a personal noun to express a plural. For example, 老师们 (lǎo shī men) means "teachers". However, if there are numeral measure words or other words implying the plural before the noun, the suffix 们 (men) can't be added to the noun. For example, we can't say 五个学生们 (wǔ gè xué shēng men), and should say 五个学生 (wǔ gè xué shēng) instead.

Generally, a noun can serve as a subject, object, attributive, or predicate in a sentence. Let's read some examples one by one.

1. As a subject:

北京是中国的首都（běi jīng shì zhōng guó de shǒu dū）。

Beijing is the capital of China.

冬天冷，夏天热（dōng tiān lěng, xià tiān rè）。

In winter it is cold; in summer it is hot.

东边是操场（dōng biān shì cāo chǎng）。

The playground is to the east.

教授给我们上课（jiào shòu gěi wǒ men shàng kè）。

The professor taught us a course.

2. As an object:

彼得正在看书（bǐ dé zhèng zài kàn shū）。

Peter is reading books.

现在五点了 (xiàn zài wǔ diǎn le)。

It is now five o'clock.

我家在北边 (wǒ jiā zài běi biān)。

My house is to the north.

她不想写作业 (tā bù xiǎng xiě zuò yè)。

She doesn't want to do her homework.

3. As an attributive with or without 的 (de) indicating attribution or possession:

我喜欢秋天的夜晚 (wǒ xǐ huān qiū tiān de yè wǎn)。

I like the night in autumn.

中文语法并不难 (zhōng wén yǔ fǎ bìng bù nán)。

Chinese grammar is not difficult.

这是德国产品 (zhè shì dé guó chǎn pǐn)。

This is a product from Germany.

4. As a predicate:

今天晴天（jīn tiān qíng tiān）。

Today is a sunny day.

昨天周一（zuó tiān zhōu yī）。

Yesterday was Monday.

5. Time nouns (indicating date, times, seasons, etc) and nouns of locality (those showing the direction to a location) can also serve as adverbial adjuncts, whereas nouns of other kinds cannot. For example:

他后天来（tā hòu tiān lái）。

He will arrive the day after tomorrow.

我们晚上上课（wǒ men wǎn shàng shàng kè）。

We have classes in the evening.

您这边请（nín zhè biān qǐng）。

This way please.

请外边抽烟（qǐng wài biān chōu yān）。

Please smoke outside.

Pronouns

Pronouns are the words that stand for nouns, verbs, adjectives, numerals, and adverbs. Chinese pronouns are classified as:

1. A pronoun which refers to persons or things is called a personal pronoun. Personal pronouns cannot be reduplicated, and they cannot take words of other parts of speech as prepositioned modifiers. For example:

我（wǒ）I, me

你（nǐ）you

他（tā）he, him

她（tā）she, her

我们（wǒ men）we, us

你们（nǐ men）you

咱们（zán men）we, us

2. A pronoun which is used to distinguish people or things is called a demonstrative pronoun. For example:

这（zhè）here

那（nà）there

3. A pronoun which is used to indicate interrogation is called an interrogative pronoun. For example:

谁（shuí）who, whom

什么（shén me）what

哪里（nǎ lǐ）where

多少（duō shǎo）how much

怎么（zěn me）how

Pronouns serve basically the same function as the words which they subsitute. Therefore, a pronoun can serve as a subject, object, attributive, adverbial adjunct, predicate, or a complement.

Adjectives

Words that describe the shape or property of a person or thing, the state of a movement, or action are called adjectives. Most adjectives can be modified by adverbs of degree. The negative adverb 不 (bù) is placed before an adjective to achieve their negative form.

Adjectives include the following kinds:

1. Describing shape, for example:

大（dà）big, large, wide, old

小（xiǎo）small, young

高（gāo）tall

矮（ǎi）short 美丽（měi lì）beautiful

帅（shuài）handsome

2. Describing the property of quality, for example:

好（hǎo）good, well

坏（huài）bad, spoiled

冷（lěng）cold

热（rè）hot

对（duì）right

错（cuò）wrong

正确（zhèng què）correct

伟大（wěi dà）great

优秀（yōu xiù）outstanding, excellent

严重（yán zhòng）serious, critical, grave, severe

3. Describing the state of a movement or action, for example:

快（kuài）fast, quick, swift

慢（màn）slow

紧张（jǐn zhāng）nervous

流利（liú lì）fluent

认真（rèn zhēn）earnest, serious

熟练（shú liàn）proficient, skilled

残酷（cán kù）cruel

In Chinese, adjectives have many functions in a sentence. Let's analyze them one by one.

1. Adjectives are mainly used as modifying attributives.

她穿了一件红裙子（tā chuān le yí jiàn hóng qún zi）。

She's wearing a red skirt.

他戴了一顶黑帽子（tā dài le yì dǐng hēi mào zi）。

He's wearing a black hat.

在乡下可以观赏宽广的原野（zài xiāng xià kě yǐ guān shǎng kuān guǎng de yuán yě）。

You can enjoy the vast expanse of the countryside fields.

我喜欢蔚蓝的天空和明媚的阳光（wǒ xǐ huān wèi lán de tiān kōng hé míng mèi de yáng guāng）。

I enjoy the blue sky and bright sunshine.

2. An adjective can serve as a predicate.

我们的时间非常紧迫（wǒ men de shí jiān fēi cháng jǐn pò）。

We have a very tight schedule.

她很漂亮（tā hěn piào liàng）。

She's very pretty.

他很矮（tā hěn ǎi）。

He's short.

百合花很香（bǎi hé huā hěn xiāng）。

Lilys are very fragrant.

3. Another of the important uses of adjectives is placed before a verb as an adverbial adjunct.

她高兴地走了（tā gāo xìng de zǒu le）。

She left happily.

他正在大声地叫喊（tā zhèng zài de shēng dì jiào hǎn）。

He's shouting loudly.

我可以流利地说中文（wǒ kě yǐ liú lì de shuō zhōng wén）。

I can speak Chinese fluently.

4. Adjectives often serve as complements to predicate verbs.

把你的衣服擦干净（bǎ nǐ de yī fu cā gàn jìng）。

Clean your clothes.

风吹干了衣服（fēng chuī gān le yī fu）。

The wind dried the clothes.

5. An adjective can serve as a subject.

谦虚是中国的传统美德（qiān xū shì zhōng guó de chuán tǒng měi dé）。

Modesty is a traditional virtue in Chinese culture.

骄傲使人落后（jiāo ào shǐ rén luò hòu）。

Pride will make you fall behind.

6. An adjective can serve as an object.

我喜欢安静（wǒ xǐ huān ān jìng）。

I like the quiet.

女孩子爱漂亮（nǚ hái zi ài piào liàng）。

Girls love being pretty.

Chapter 3: Verbs and Auxiliary Verbs

Verbs

Words indicating actions, behavior, mental activities, changes and development, etc. are called verbs. Verbs can be grouped into transitive verbs and intransitive verbs according to whether they take an object. Verbs that can be followed immediately by an object are called transitive verbs. Verbs that can't immediately take an object are called intransitive verbs. Verbs can be negated by the negative adverbs 不（bù）, 没（méi）, or 没有（méi yǒu）.

1. As a predicate

我喜欢旅游（wǒ xǐ huān lǚ yóu）。

I like travelling.

她坐在椅子上（tā zuò zài yǐ zi shàng）。

She's sitting on a chair.

2. As a subject

A verb can be used as a subject on the condition that the predicate of the sentence is an adjective or a verb expressing the ideas of "stop, start, or judge".

浪费可耻（làng fèi kě chǐ）。

Waste is disgraceful.

战斗开始了（zhàn dòu kāi shǐ le）。

The fight begins.

3. As an attributive

的（de）must be added to a verb used as an attributive.

你有喝的东西吗（nǐ yǒu hē de dōng xī ma）？

Do you have something to drink?

他说的话很对（tā shuō de huà hěn duì）。

What he said is correct.

4. As an object

我喜欢游泳（wǒ xǐ huān yóu yǒng）。

I like swimming.

他们十一点结束了讨论（tā men shí yī diǎn jié shù le tǎo lùn）。

They ended the discussion at 11 o'clock.

5. As a complement

车开过来了（chē kāi guò lái le）。

The car came over.

我听得懂（wǒ tīng de dǒng）。

I understand.

6. As an adverbial adjunct

Note that only auxiliary verbs can serve as an adverbial adjunct. We will introduce you more about auxiliary verbs in the next chapter.

我们要认真对待这项工作（wǒ men yào rèn zhēn duì dài zhè xiàng gōng zuò）。

We should take this work seriously.

他会来的（tā huì lái de）。

He will come.

Here are some points that merit special attention.

1. Chinese verbs have no morphological changes whatsoever resulting from person, gender, number, time, etc.

我是医生（wǒ shì yī shēng）。

I'm a doctor.

她是护士（tā shì hù shì）。
She's a nurse.
他们是工人（tā men shì gōng rén）。
They are workers.
他正在写作业（tā zhèng zài xiě zuò yè）。
He is doing his homework.
他每天晚上写作业（tā měi tiān wǎn shàng xiě zuò yè）。
He does his homework every night.
他早就写了作业（tā zǎo jiù xiě le zuò yè）。
He did his homework earlier.

2. The particle 了 (le) is suffixed to a verb to emphasize a competed action. For example:

我写了一本书（wǒ xiě le yì běn shū）。
I finished writing a book.
她走了（tā zǒu le）。
She left.

3. The particle 着 (zhe) is suffixed to a verb to show a progressive action or continuous state. For example:

我开着车呢（wǒ kāi zhe chē ne）！
I'm currently driving (a vehicle).
窗户开着呢（chuāng hù kāi zhe ne）。
The window is opening.

4. The particle 过 (guò) is suffixed to a verb to stress on a certain experience in the past. For example:

我看过这本书（wǒ kàn guò zhè běn shū）。
I have read this book before.
他之前干过翻译（tā zhī qián gàn guò fān yì）。
He used to be a translator.

Auxiliary Verb

The Chinese language doesn't have modal verb, but verbs that "help" other verbs to express necessity, possibility, and willingness. These verbs are called auxiliary verbs. Auxiliary verbs are often used to modify verbs or adjectives, and they are negated by 不(bù). In addition, a noun cannot immediately follow them. The affirmative-negative question is formed by putting together the affirmative and negative forms of an auxiliary verb, and that question formed can be answered by the auxiliary verb directly. For example:

你能不能来（nǐ néng bù néng lái）？

Can you come or not?

能（néng）。

Yes, I can.

不能（bù néng）。

No, I cannot.

他想不想打游戏（tā xiǎng bù xiǎng dǎ yóu xì）？

Does he want to play video games or not?

想（xiǎng）。

Yes, he does.

不想（bù xiǎng）。

No, he doesn't.

Auxiliary verbs are often used as adverbial adjuncts before verbs and adjectives. Below we will introduce usage of some common anxiliary verbs.

1. Those expressing capability, for example:

能（néng）can, be capable of

我能办好这件事（wǒ néng bàn hǎo zhè jiàn shì）。

I can do this thing.

能够（néng gòu）can, be capable of, be able to

她能够做到（tā néng gòu zuò dào）。

She can make it.

会（huì）can, be able to

你会说中文吗（nǐ huì shuō zhōng wén ma）？

Can you speak Chinese?

2. Those expressing possibility, for example:

能 (néng) = may

我能进来吗（wǒ néng jìn lái ma）？
May I come in?
会（huì）will
她会来吗（tā huì lái ma）？
Will she come?
可以（kě yǐ）can, be able to
你不可以在这里吸烟（nǐ bú kě yǐ zài zhè lǐ xī yān）。
You can't smoke here.
可能（kě néng）might happen, possible, probable
天可能要下雨（tiān kě néng yào xià yǔ）。
It might rain.

3. Those expressing necessity by reason, for example:
应该（yīng gāi）ought to, should
你应该走了（nǐ yīng gāi zǒu le）。
You should leave now.
应当（yīng dāng）should, be supposed to
你不应当出现在这里（nǐ bù yīng dāng chū xiàn zài zhè lǐ）。
You are not supposed to be here.
该（gāi）should
我该吃药了（wǒ gāi chī yào le）。
I should take some medicine.
要（yào）must
我要去上班了（wǒ yào qù shàng bān le）。
I must go to work.

4. Those expressing obligation, for example:
必须（bì xū）have to, must
每个人都必须遵纪守法（měi gè rén dōu bì xū zūn jì shǒu fǎ）。
Everyone must abide by the law.
得（děi）need to, have to
你今天得把钱还给我（nǐ jīn tiān děi bǎ qián huán gěi wǒ）。

You have to pay me back today.

5. Those expressing willingness, for example:

要（yào）want to

她要去国外旅游（tā yào qù guó wài lǚ yóu）。

She wants to travel abroad.

想（xiǎng）want to, wish to

我想睡觉（wǒ xiǎng shuì jiào）。

I want to sleep.

愿意（yuàn yì）wish to, be willing to

他非常愿意做这件事（tā fēi cháng yuàn yì zuò zhè jiàn shì）。

He is very willing to do this thing.

敢（gǎn）dare to

她敢去挑战领导的权威（tā gǎn qù tiāo zhàn lǐng dǎo de quán wēi）。

She dares to challenge the authority of her supervisor.

肯（kěn）be willing to, be ready to

这孩子不肯回家（zhè hái zi bù kěn huí jiā）。

The child is unwilling to go back home.

Chapter 4: Numerals and Measure Words

Numerals

Words representing numbers are called numerals, such as: 一（yī）one

二（èr）two

三（sān）three

四（sì）four

五（wǔ）five

六（liù）six

七（qī）seven

八（bā）eight

九（jiǔ）nine

十（shí）ten

百（bǎi）hundred

千（qiān）thousand

万（wàn）ten thousand

亿（yì）a hundred million

零（líng）zero

两（liǎng）two

The above basic numerals can be combined with words to represent various kinds of numbers. Larger numbers in Chinese are especially logical.

Numbers from 11-19: 十（shí）+ number. For example: 十四（shí sì）fourteen

Multiples of 10: number + 十（shí）. For example: 五十（wǔ shí）fifty

From 21-29: 二十（èr shí）+ number. For example: 二十三（èr shí sān）twenty-three, and so forth. The same applies to larger numbers, for example 七十六（qī shí liù）seventy-six.

Hundreds: 100 is 一百（yī bǎi）, 200 is 两百（liǎng bǎi）, 300 is 三百（sān bǎi）, and so forth.

Thousands: 1,000 is 一千 (yì qiān), 2,000 is 两千 (liǎng qiān), 3,000 is 三千 (sān qiān), and so forth.

Chinese has two words for "two".

èr is used in counting and in words for larger numbers. For example: 二十二（èr shí èr）twenty-two.

liǎng is used when you are talking about two of something. For example: 两个苹果（liǎng gè píng guǒ）two apples.

The 2 in numbers from 20-29 is always èr. While the 2 in numbers like 200 and 2,000 can either.

Ordinal numbers can be formed by placing the prefix 第（dì）before numerals. For example:

第一（dì yī）first

第十（dì shí）tenth

In some circumstances, however, numerals can bu put directly before nouns to act as ordinal numbers. For example:

三楼（sān lóu）the third floor

二哥（èr gē）second brother

Multiple numbers are formed by adding the measure word 倍（bèi）after numerals. For example:

一倍（yí bèi）one time

二十倍（èr shí bèi）twenty times

一千倍（yì qiān bèi）a thousand times

Decimals are shown by the formula number + 点（diǎn）+ number. The numbers before 点（diǎn）are the whole number and the figures after 点（diǎn）are the decimal places. For example:

零点三（líng diǎn sān）zero point three

十点七五（shí diǎn qī wǔ）ten point seventy five

Chinese uses number + 分之（fēn zhī）+ number to indicate fractions. The denominator is placed before the numerator. For example:

三分之二（sān fēn zhī èr）two thirds

十分之九（shí fēn zhī jiǔ）nine tenths

Now, let's have a tongue twister.

四是四，十是十 (sì shì sì, shí shì shí)。

十四是十四，四十是四十 (shí sì shì shí sì, sì shí shì sì shí)。

谁说十四是四，就打谁十四 (shuí shuō shí sì shì sí sì, jiù dǎ shuí shí sì)。

谁说四十是十，就打谁四十 (shuí shuō sì shí shì shì shí, jiù dǎ shuí sì shí)。

Fun, isn't it? Well, we don't provide translation here because this is only a tongue twister to entertain! If you want to figure out what this short tongue twister means, just keep studying this book with us!

Measure words

In Chinese, there is a special part of speech known as the measure word. It indicates the measure or unit of things or persons. In modern Chinese, a numeral may not qualify a noun by itself; there must be a measure word between the numeral and the noun. Almost everything can be "measured", represented by a specific measure word. Therefore, it is imperative for foreign learners of Chinese to learn every noun with its matching measure word.

There are over two hundred measure words in Chinese. Normally people choose the measure word according to the appearance of the object. Some of the most important measure words are:

个（gè）

Used before a noun which does not have a fixed measure word of its own. It is the most common and multi-purpose nominal measure word. For example:

一个人（yí gè rén）one person

两个桔子（liǎng gè jú zi）two oranges

三个苹果（sān gè píng guǒ）three apples

种（zhǒng）kind, sort, type

这里有三种果汁（zhè lǐ yǒu sān zhǒng guǒ zhī）。
There are three types of juice.

我想买这种杯子（wǒ xiǎng mǎi zhè zhǒng bēi zi）。
I want to buy this kind of cup.

我不做那种工作（wǒ bú zuò nà zhǒng gōng zuò）。
I don't do that kind of work.

些，一些（xiē, yì xiē）some

这些（zhè xiē）these

那些（nà xiē）those

我要去超市买些水果（wǒ yào qù chāo shì mǎi xiē shuǐ guǒ）。
I need to buy some fruit from the supermarket.

你能不能借我一些钱（nǐ néng bù néng jiè wǒ yì xiē qián）？
Could you please lend me some money?

我不喜欢那些人（wǒ bù xǐ huān nà xiē rén）。
I don't like those people.

瓶（píng）bottle

一瓶水（yì píng shuǐ）a bottle of water

两瓶可乐（liǎng píng kě lè）two bottles of coke.

杯（bēi）cup

一杯茶（yì bēi chá）a cup of tea

三杯咖啡（sān bēi kā fēi）three cups of coffee

条（tiáo）

Used to describe something long, narrow, or thin. For example:

一条围巾（yì tiáo wéi jīn）a scarf

一条路（yì tiáo lù）a path

块（kuài）piece, lump

两块面包（liǎng kuài miàn bāo）two pieces of bread

几块冰（jǐ kuài bīng）a few pieces of ice

袋，包（dài，bāo）bag

两袋盐（liǎng dài yán）two bags of salt

四包饼干（sì bāo bǐng gān）four bags of cookies

本（běn）

Used to describe books, magazines, notebooks, etc. For example:

一本字典（yì běn zì diǎn）a dictionary

两本杂志（liǎng běn zá zhì）too magazines

张（zhāng）

Used to describe something with a flat surface. For example:

一张桌子（yì zhāng zhuō zi）a table

一张床（yì zhāng chuáng）a bed

Next, we will introduce you to the proper way to count Chinese money and express time.

The Chinese currency is Renminbi (RMB or CNY) and has two units: 元（yuán）or 块（kuài）and 角（jiǎo）or 毛（máo）.

元（yuán）is always used after an amount of money written in Arabic numerals. For example:

0.5元，0.5元钱，5角钱（líng diǎn wǔ yuán, líng diǎn wǔ yuán qián, wǔ jiǎo qián）50 cents

6.8 元，6.8 元钱，6 元 8 角钱（liù diǎn bā yuán, liù diǎn bā yuán qián, liù yuán bā jiǎo qián）6 yuan and 80 cents

In spoken Chinese, the 钱（qián）in the above examples is often omitted. Moreover, 块（kuài）and 毛（máo）are more used in spoken Chinese and the last measure word can be omitted. For example:

五毛（wǔ máo）fifty cents

六块八（liù kuài bā）six *yuan* and eighty cents

To express time, Chinese has 年（nián），月（yuè），周（zhōu），星期（xīng qī），礼拜（lǐ bài），and 日（rì）or 号（hào）.

To indicate years, the pattern is: number + 年（nián）

For example:

今年是二零二零年（jīn nián shì èr líng èr líng nián）。

This year is 2020.

这个国家有两千年历史（zhè gè guó jiā yǒu liǎng qiān nián lì shǐ）。

This country has a history of 2,000 years.

For months of the year, the pattern is: number + 月（yuè）

一月（yī yuè）January

二月（èr yuè）February

三月（sān yuè）March

四月（sì yuè）April

五月（wǔ yuè）May

六月（liù yuè）June

七月（qī yuè）July

八月（bā yuè）August

九月（jiǔ yuè）September

十月（shí yuè）October

十一月（shí yī yuè）November

十二月（shí èr yuè）December

Names for days of the week are formed using the pattern 星期（xīng qī）+ number, 礼拜（lǐ bài）+ number, or 周（zhōu）+ number. Sunday is an exception.

星期一（xīng qī yī）Monday
星期二（xīng qī èr）Tuesday
星期三（xīng qī sān）Wednesday
星期四（xīng qī sì）Thursday
星期五（xīng qī wǔ）Friday
星期六（xīng qī liù）Saturday
星期天（xīng qī tiān）Sunday

For all of the above, 周（zhōu）or 礼拜（lǐ bài）can be substituted for 星期（xīng qī）.

To express date, the pattern is number + 日（rì）or 号（hào）. 号（hào）is more common in colloquial language. For example:

今天是一月十一号（jīn tiān shì yī yuè shí yī hào）。
Today is January 11th.

今天是二月十二日（jīn tiān shì èr yuè shí èr rì）。
Today is Feburary 12th.

In Chinese, a date is given in the following order: Year-Month-Date. Therefore, if you want to express your birthday, you should say:

我的生日是1995年2月28日（wǒ de shēng rì shì yī jiǔ jiǔ wǔ nián èr yuè èr shí bā rì）。
I was born on Feb 28th, 1995.

Chapter 5: Auxiliary Words

Chinese words can be divided into two categories according to their meaning and grammatical function – notional words and auxiliary words. Notional words have actual meaning and can act as independent sentence elements. We already learned about notional words in Chapter 2 to 4. Auxiliary words do not have actual meaning and can not be used alone as sentence elements. Adverbs, prepositions, conjunctions, particles, interjections, and onamatopes are in this category. The use of auxiliary words plays an important role in the Chinese language. Though these words do not carry concrete lexical meaning, they are grammatically important. Let's discuss them one by one.

Adverbs

A word generally used in front of a verb or adjective to express time, degree, scope, repetition, negation, possibility, or tone of speech, etc. is called an adverb. Adverbs cannot be used as modifier of a noun or be reduplicated. Moreover, most of them cannot be used alone to answer a question or precede subjects.

The basic use of an adverb is to serve as adverbial adjunct. As an adverbial adjunct, the adverb is always placed before a verb or an adjective and never after. For example:

他今天特别高兴（tā jīn tiān tè bié gāo xìng）。
He's really happy today.
这个女孩真漂亮（zhè gè nǚ hái zhēn piào liàng）。
This girl is very ptetty.

Prepositons

A word that can be put before a noun or pronoun to form a prepositional phrase indicating time, place, direction, object, reason, manner, passive, comparison, or exclusion, etc. is called a preposition. Generally speaking, a preposition cannot be an element of a sentence by itself. Most prepositions must take a noun or a pronoun to form a prepositional phrase to serve as an adverbial adjunct, complement or attributive, for example:

As an adverbial adjunct:
他从北方来（tā cóng běi fāng lái）。
He's from the north.

As an attributive:
这是关于月亮的传说（zhè shì guān yú yuè liàng de chuán shuō）。
This legend is about moon.

As a complement:
这列火车开往深圳（zhè liè huǒ chē kāi wǎng shēn zhèn）。
This train is heading toward Shenzhen.

Conjunctions

A conjunction is a word that can be joined with two words, phrases, or sentences to indicate the grammatical relation of coordination, causality, condition, supposition, etc. For example:

Coordination:
和，跟，同，与，及，并（hé, gēn, tóng, yǔ, jí, bìng）and

Causality:
因为（yīn wèi）because
所以（suǒ yǐ）so
因此（yīn cǐ）therefore

Condition:
只要（zhī yào）as long as
只有（zhī yǒu）only
不管（bù guǎn）despite

Supposition
如果，要是，假如，假设（rú guǒ, yào shì, jiǎ rú, jiǎ shè）if

Inference:
既然（jì rán）since, now that
这样（zhè yàng）like this
那么（nà me）in that way

Transition:
虽然（suī rán）though
但是（dàn shì）but
可是，不过（kě shì, bú guò）however

Concession:
即使（jí shǐ）even if

Alternative:
还是，或者（hái shì, huò zhě）or

Enumeration:
例如（lì rú）for example
比如（bǐ rú）such as

Succession:
接着，然后（jiē zhe, rán hòu）then

Progression:
甚至（shèn zhì）even

Particles

A word which is added to another word, phrase, or sentence to indicate various supplementary meanings, grammatical relations, or mood is called a particle. Particles can be divided into three kinds.

1. Structural particles

Particles added to words or phrases to indicate grammatical relations are called structural particles. The most important structural particles are:

的（de）as in 我的书（wǒ de shū）my book.

地（de）as in 高兴地说（gāo xìng de shuō）happily say

得（de）as in 跑得快（pǎo de kuài）run fast

2. Aspectual particles

Particles added to verbs to indicate a supplementary meaning are called aspectual particles. The aspectual particles are:

了（le）

Suffixed to a verb indicating the completion of an action.

他走了（tā zǒu le）。

He left.

着（zhe）

Indicates that an action is in progress or in a certain state at a certain time, or a certain state is continuing.

她在房间唱着歌（tā zài fáng jiān chàng zhe gē）。

She's singing in the room.

过（guo）

Indicates that an action took place in the past.

我去过美国（wǒ qù guo měi guó）。

I have been to America.

3. Modal particles

Particles used at the end of a sentence to express moods are:

吗（ma）呢（ne）吧（ba）啊（a）嘛（ma）啦（la）呀（ya）哇（wa）

When not knowing something and expecting an answer, the speaker can put 吗（ma）at the end of a statement. For example:

你好吗（nǐ hǎo ma）？

How are you?

抽屉里有笔吗（chōu tì lǐ yǒu bǐ ma）？

Is there any pen in the drawer?

呢（ne）can be used at the end of an affirmative-negative sentence to indicate a tone of uncertainty. For example:

她能不能来呢（tā néng bù néng lái ne）？

Will she be able to come?

呢（ne）can be used at the end of a question with an interrogative pronoun to indicate a tone of conjecture. For example:

这是谁的书呢（zhè shì shuí de shū ne）？

Whose book is this?

呢（ne）can be used at the end of an alternative question to suggest a tone of releasing or urging.

你喜欢英语还是喜欢法语呢（nǐ shì xué yīng yǔ hái shì xué fǎ yǔ ne）？

Do you like English or French?

Interjections

An interjection is a word which can express an exclamation, a call or a reponse. It doesn't have a concrete meaning. It only indicates a kind of feeling or a sound that draws attention. Interjections are quite independent and have no grammatical relationships with other parts of the sentence. They usually occur at the beginning of a sentence. For example:

喂（wèi）嗯（èn）啊（á，à）哎（āi）噢（ō）哦（ò）唉（ài）

Each interjection expresses a certain feeling or imitates a certain sound, so it cannot be used indiscriminately. Here are some interjection use cases:

喂（wèi）is used when answering a phone call.

嗯（èn）indicates response.

啊（á）indicates surprise.

啊（à）indicates admiration.

哎（āi）is used when friends say hello to each other.

噢（ō）or 哦（ò）indicates realization and awakening.

唉（ài）is the sound of a sigh.

Onomatopes

An onomatope is a word which imitates the sound of a thing or an action. It doesn't have concrete meaning but only indicates a sound. For example:

哗哗（huá huá）thesound of water flowing

哈哈（hā hā）the sound of laughter

呼呼（hū hū）the sound of wind

汪汪（wāng wāng）dogs barking

扑通（pū tōng）sound of a big weight falling onto the ground or into the water

Section 2: GRAMMAR

Chapter 6: Phrases and Sentence Elements

Phrases

A sentence is composed of words and phrases. Phrases are combinations of grammatically related words, and like words, function as sentence elements. Some phrases can also stand alone as a sentence. Phrases are sometimes called construtions. There are a variety of phrases in Chinese, of which the following 11 are commonly used:

1. The coordinative phrase

A coordinative phrase is one formed by two or more words of the same part of speech in coordinative relation. The order of the two constituents is not fixed. Reversion of the order does not affect the meaning. A coordinative phrase is usually composed of nouns, pronouns, verbs, or adjectives. For example:

老师学生（lǎo shī xué shēng）teachers and students

他和我（tā hé wǒ）he and I

又唱又跳（yòu chàng yòu tiào）sing and dance

高大帅气（gāo dà shuài qì）tall and handsome

2. The subject-predicate phrase

A subject-predicate phrase is one in which the constituents are combined in the relation. The order of the two constituents is fixed with the subject preceding the predicate. The first constituent of the phrase is usually a noun or pronoun serving as a topic or the subject, and the second one, usually a verb or an adjective, is the predicate describing the subject. The resersion of order will bring about a change both in structure and in meaning. For example:

头发长（tóu fa cháng）hair is long

长头发（cháng tóu fa）long hair

目的明确（mù de míng què）the destination is clear

明确目的（míng què mù de）to know the destination

3. The verb-object phrase

A verb-pbject phrase is one in which the constituents are combined in the relation. The order of constituents of the phase is fixed, and the verb precedes the object. For example:

吃早饭（chī zǎo fàn）eat breakfast

写汉字（xiě hàn zi）write Chinese character

4. The endocentric phrase

An endocentric phrase is one in which the constituents are combined so that the first modifies the second, and the order of the two constituents can not be reversed. The reversion of order will lead to a change both in structure and in meaning, or even make the phrase logically or grammatically unsound. For example:

很结实（hěn jié shi）very strong

太晚（tài wǎn）too late

他哥哥（tā gē ge）his older brother

5. The numeral-measure phrase

A phrase which is the combination of a numeral and a measure word is called a numeral-measure word phrase. The order of the two constituents in the phrase is fixed: the numeral always precedes the measure word, and this order cannot be reversed. For example:

三本书（sān běn shū）three books

两支笔（liǎng zhī bǐ）two pens

However, one can say 书三本（shū sān běn）or 笔两支（bǐ liǎng zhī）in statistics.

6. The complementary phrase

A complementary phrase is one in which the constituents are combined in a complementary relationship. It can be formed by a verb and its complement or an adjective and its complement. The complement may be a verb, adjective, and in a few cases, an adverb or a phrase. The order of the two constituents in the phrase is fixed. For example:

感觉真棒（gǎn jué zhēn bàng）feel great

危险得很（wēi xiǎn de hěn）incredibly dangerous

7. The locality phrase

The phrase of locality is one where the noun of locality is a modified word indicating place, position, time, or quantity. The order of the two constituents can not be reversed, for the reversion will lead to a change of meaning. For example:

三天前（sān tiān qián）three days before

前三天（qián sān tiān）the first three days

屋里（wū lǐ）in the room

里屋（lǐ wū）the inner room

8. The appositive phrase

A combination of two words which refer to the same person or thing from different aspects, and where each adds some information to the other is called an appositive phrase. The order of the two constituents is fixed, with the emphasis on the second one. For example:

你们三个（nǐ men sān gè）you three

我朋友保罗（wǒ péng yǒu bǎo luó）my friend Paul

9. The set phrase

A set phrase, such as a proper noun, a technical term, an idiom, etc. is one which is composed of fixed constituents to express a specific concept and is used as a while. None of the constituents in a set phrase can be substituted and they are arranged in a fixed order. For example:

有其父必有其子（yǒu qí fù bì yǒu qí zǐ）like father like son

爱屋及乌（ài wū jí wū）love me love my dog

中华人民共和国（zhōng huá rén mín gòng hé guó）The People's Republic of China

了如指掌（liǎo rú zhǐ zhǎng）to know something like the palm of one's hand

开诚布公（kāi chéng bù gōng）to speak frankly and sincerely

10. The prepositional phrase

The prepositional phrase is formed by a preposition and its object. It refers to directions, place, position, time, object, purpose, reason, or maner of an action, and expresses passivity, comparison, disposal, or exclusion etc. The word order of a prepositional phrase is fixed: the preposition always precedes its object. Nouns, pronouns, numeral-measure phrase, nouns, phrases of locality, time nouns, or nominal endocentric phrases can serve as a prepositonal object. For example:

除了这座城市（chú le zhè zuò chéng shì）except this city

在网上（zài wǎng shàng）on the internet

从美国（cóng měi guó）from America

11. The 的（de）phrase

The 的（de）phrase is one in which the structural particle 的（de）is attached to a notional word or phrase which refers to a person or thing. In the phrase, as a rule, 的（de）must be suffixed to the other constituent. The phrase functions as a noun in a sentence. For example:

这是他给我的（zhè shì tā gěi wǒ de）。

He gave me this.

他给我的是一本书（tā gěi wǒ de shì yì běn shū）。

What he gave me is a book.

她是来参加表演的（tā shì lái cān jiā biǎo yǎn de）。

She is coming for the show.

参加表演的在里面（cān jiā biǎo yǎn de zài lǐ miàn）。

Those coming to the show are inside.

All in all, we distinguish the various phrases according to the following features:

1. In terms of parts of speech, grammatical relations, and meanings of their constituents.

2. In terms of whether their constituents are arranged in a fixed order.

3. In terms of the ways in which their constituents are connected, ie. Whether conjunctions are employed and if so, what kind of conjunctions are employed.

4. In terms of whether the phrase can be preceded or followed by other elements and what these elements are.

Sentence Elements

A sentence is the smallest language unit of communication that can be used by itself to express an idea. Sentences are composed of words and phrases arranged according to certain grammatical relationships which can include several sentence elements in line with their syntax functions. Generally, there are six sentence elements: subject, predicate, object, attributive, adverbial adjunct, and complement. Words or phrases can act as sentence elements. Do you remember how many kinds of Chinese words and phrases we've learned above?

1. Subject

In Chinese, the subject of a sentence is determined by its position and meaning. Usually the subject, which is the theme of a statement, occurs at the beginning of a sentence before the predicate. There is not any particular marker for the subject in Chinese. Words or phrases can serve as subjects with out any change in form, even verbs or verbal phrases functioning as subject are not market by any words such as pronouns etc., and the form of the verbs will remain unchanged. For example:

学习中文很有意思（xué xí zhōng wén hěn yǒu yì si）。

Learning Chinese is very interesting.

受人帮助道谢是一种礼节（shòu rén bāng zhù dào xiè shì yì zhǒng lǐ jié）。

It is polite to say thanks to those that help you.

Another important feature is that subjects in most sentences are doers of actions, the ones that launch the action. But there are some other cases, instead of launching the action, the subjects receive the actions, they are the receivers of actions. Such cases are common in Chinese, and they do not have to be a passive sentence.

房间打扫干净了（fáng jiān dǎ sǎo gàn jìng le）。

The room has been cleaned.

作业写完了（zuò yè xiě wán le）。

The homework has been finished.

2. Predicate

Relationships between a subject and predicate are various. The predicate indicates an action done or received by the subject, describes, explains, or makes a judgement of the subject, expressing what the subject is, what it does, or how it is. For example:

她是我妻子（tā shì wǒ qī zi）。

She's my wife.

树叶黄了（shù yè huáng le）。

The leaves are turning yellow.

玛丽又迟到了（mǎ lì yòu chí dào le）。

Mary is late again.

3. Object

There are various relationships between the object and verb predicates. In terms of meaning and function, the object can be the doer or receiver of an action, the result or influence of an action, the destination of an action, or the instrument with which an action is done.

Words or phrases are used as objects without any morphological marker. With verbs, verb-object phrases, coordinative or endocentric verbal phrases, or subject-predicate phrases function as the object, no preposition or pronoun is required and the verb in these phrases remains unchanged in form this is very important. For example:

我们需要休息（wǒ men xū yào xiū xi）。

We need to take a rest.

我需要休息一会儿（wǒ xū yào xiū xi yì huìr）。

I need to rest for a while.

Some verbs take two objects, which are called double objects. The first one, mostly a personal noun or pronoun, is called an indirect object and the second one, mostly a noun or phrase of non-personal reference, is called a direct object. For example:

我送她一件礼物（wǒ sòng tā yí jiàn lǐ wù）。

I gave her a present.

她教我们英语（tā jiāo wǒ men yīng yǔ）。

She teaches us English.

You may notice that in the above examples no auxiliary word is used between the two objects, but their order is fixed: the indirect object (referring to person) is followed by the direct object (of non-personal reference).

In Chinese, most objects are receivers of actions, but some objects are the active doers of actions. Objects that do actions often appear in such sentences: beginning words or phrases denoting place or time are used to indicate the existence, appearance, or disappearance of a thing or a person. If the objects are people, living animals, or plants, they are objects that do actions. For example:

昨天我家来了两位客人（zuó tiān wǒ jiā lái le liǎng wèi kè rén）。

Yesterday my home came two guests. (I had two guests visiting me yesterday.)

门口站着一个人（mén kǒu zhàn zhe yí gè rén）。

By the door is standing a person. (There is a person standing by the door.)

4. Attributive

A word or phrase which modifies or restricts the subject or object is called an attributive and the word modified by the attributibe is called the head word. In other words, the attributive is the premodifier showing the property, quality, quantity, category, place, time, or scope of what is denoted by the head word. It must be noted that the attributive must be placed before the head word it modifies and this order cannot be reversed, as the reversion of order will lead to a change of structure and meaning, or will even make the phrase senseless. For example:

左边的房子（zuǒ biān de fáng zi）the house on the left

房子的左边（fáng zi de zuǒ biān）on the left of the house

厚外套（hòu wài tào）thick coat

外套厚（wài tào hòu）the coat is thick

今天的报纸（jīn tiān de bào zhǐ）today's newspaper

5. Adverbial adjunct

A word or phrase modifying or restricting a predicate is called an adverbial adjunct and the word it modifies is the head word. In other words, the adverbial adjunct is the premodifying element denoting the time, place, degree, scope, aspect, affirmation or negation, repetition, activeness or passiveness, target, reason, etc. of the head word. What should be noted is that adverbial adjuncts must precede, not follow, the head words which they modify or restrict. For example:

他不喜欢打篮球（tā bù xǐ huān dǎ lán qiú）。

He doesn't like to play basketball.

我们用汉语交流（wǒ men yòng hàn yǔ jiāo liú）。

We communicate with each other in Chinese.

Two or more adverbs are often used in succession as adverbial adjuncts. When thus used, attention should be paid to their order: the modifier always precedes the modified and this order can not be reversed. Otherwise, the meaning will be changed, become illogical, or ungrammatical. For example:

十年前的这件事我已经不记得了（shí nián qián de zhè jiàn shì wǒ yǐ jīng bú jì dé le）。

I don't remember the thing happened ten years ago.

很多大学生都经常兼职（hěn duō dà xué shēng dōu jīng cháng jiān zhí）。

Many college students often take part time jobs.

6. Complement

A word or phrase attached to a verb or adjective predicate to complete the meaning is called a complement. Complements are postmodifying elements to show the duration, quantity, degree, result, direction or possibility of an action; or to illustrate the state, number, degree of a thing.

The grammatical feathres of complements are: the complement always comes after the head word; mainly adjectives, vers, numeral-measure word phrases, complementary phrases, etc. can act as complements; the structural particle 得（de）often occurs between the head word and the complement; uaually a verb predicate with a complement can take an object.

In terms of both meaning and structure, complements can be classified into five types: result, degree, quantity, direction, and potentiality.

Chapter 7: Simple and Complex Sentences

A sentence is composed of words or phrases arranged according to certain grammatical rules to express a comparatively complete meaning along with certain tones and intonations. In connected discourse, there is a stop between each two sentences which is indicated by a full stop in writing. Sentences can be divided into two categories: simple and complex.

Simple Sentences

A simple sentence usually consists of two sections: the subject section and the predicate section, with the former preceding the latter. It may contain one word, several words, or phrases.

Senctences can be classified, in terms of whether they contain one or two sections, into the subject-predicate sentences and the non-subject-predicate sentences.

A sentence containing the subject section and the predicate section is called a subject-predicate sentence. For example:

这里真安静（zhè lǐ zhēn ān jìng）。

It's really quiet here.

他们是交换生（tā men shì jiāo huàn shēng）。

They're an exchange student.

A sentence is called a non-subject-predicate if it does not contain or cannot be divided into the subject and the predicate sections. For example:

人呢（rén ne）？

Anyone here?

看（kàn）！

Look!

禁止吸烟（jìn zhǐ xī yān）。

No smoking.

The simple sentence expresses different meanings and tones such as a declaration, interrogation, etc. Sentences can be classified in terms of function and tone into four types: declarative, interrogative, imperative and exclamatory.

The declarative sentence is one used to state a thing or view. The sentence is uttered in the declarative tone and a full stop is written at the end. The declarative sentence may be one in the subject-predicate structure or in the non-subject-predicate structure. For example:

这是我的车（zhè shì wǒ de chē）。

This is my car.

今天天气真好（jīn tiān tiān qì zhēn hǎo）。

Today is a fine day.

开始（kāi shǐ）！

Begin!

An interrogative sentence is one used to ask a question, or a sentence uttered in the interrogative tone with a question mark written at the end. There are five major types of interrogative sentences:

1. Yes or no question: expecting yes or no as its answer. For example:

这是你的吗（zhè shì nǐ de ma）？

Is this yours?

2. Questions using interrogative pronouns: ask about a specific person, object, or other thing. For example:

他去哪里了（tā qù nǎ lǐ le）？

Where is he?

3. Affirmative and negative questions: formed by putting the affirmative and negative forms of the predicate together. Answers expected are either affirmative or negative. For example:

你要不要买这个（nǐ yào bú yào mǎi zhè ge）？

Will you buy this or not?

4. Alternative questions: questions in which several alternatives are paralleled by the conjunction 还是（hái shì） for the answerer to choose. For example:

你喜欢这红色的外套还是黑色得（nǐ xǐ huān zhè hóng sè de wài tào hái shì hēi sè de）？

Which coat do you like? The red one or the black one?

5. Rhetorical questions: questions to retort or to exaggerate. For example:

他不是个老师吗（tā bú shì ge lǎo shī ma）？

He is a teacher, isn't he?

The imperative sentence is one that expresses a command, request, urging, advice, warning, or consultation and has an imperative tone. At the end of such a sentence, a full stop or an exclamation mark is used. The subject is often absent in an imperative sentence. For example:

请进（qǐng jìn）。

Please come in.

快点（kuài diǎn）！

Hurry up!

The exclamatory sentence is a sentence that expresses praise, fondness, surprise, detestation, etc. and has an exclamatory tone. The exclamation mark is used at the end. Adverbs expressing high degrees such as 多么（duō me），真（zhēn），太（tài），etc.

are often used in an exclamatory sentence as adverbial adjuncts or complements. For example:

这城市真大（zhè chéng shì zhēn dà）！

What a big city this is!

我太累了（wǒ tài lèi le）！

I'm so tired!

Complex sentences

Sentences consisting of two or more simple sentences, expressing a complete meaning and spoken in a certain intonation are called complex sentences. Simple sentences contained in a complex sentence are called clasues. Complex sentences can also be very simple, and simple sentences can be complex too. For example:

你刚走，她就来了（nǐ gāng zǒu, tā jiù lái le）。

She came just when you left.

风停了，雨也不下了（fēng tíng le, yǔ yě bú xià le）。

When the wind stopped, the rain stopped.

A complex sentence contains two or more clauses between which there is a pause. The pause is indicated by a comma or sometimes by a semicolon in writing. When the whole sentence is spoken, there should be a stop which is indicated in writing by a full stop, a question mark, or an exclamation mark. The sentence is spoken intonationally as a complete whole.

The clauses in a complex sentence may be various kinds of subject-predicate sentences. If the clauses share the same subject, then the subject does not have to be repeated. Some complex sentences may not have subject. For example:

她会英语，她还会法语（tā huì yīng yǔ, tā hái huì fǎ yǔ）。

She can speak English, and also speak French.

这本小说没意思，我不想看了（zhè běn xiǎo shuō méi yì si, wǒ bù xiǎng kàn le）。

This novel is boring. I don't want to read it.

他今天很忙，不能陪你出去（tā jīn tiān hěn máng, bù néng péi nǐ chū qù）。

He is too busy to go out with you today.

In a complex sentence, clauses have various relationships which are often denoted by correlatives. For example:

因为今天是周末，所以公园里人特别多（yīn wéi jīn tiān shì zhōu mò, suǒ yǐ gōng yuán lǐ rén tè bié duō）。

Because today is the weekend, there are a lot of people at the park.

我们不仅要好好学习，还要锻炼好身体（wǒ men bù jǐn yào hǎo hǎo xué xí, hái yào duàn liàn hǎo shēn tǐ）。

We must not only study hard, but also exercise well.

Section 3: CONVERSATION

Conversation is the heart of language learning. Talking with someone in another language develops your listening skills while giving you the speaking practice that you need. Conversing in another language can be hard to manage when are first starting out. In this section, not only will we guide, but also your language partner as well. Conversation is all about improvising within the linguistc and cultural rules of the language. This part allows you to improvise with a manageable number of high frequency questions and answers and gives your language partner a guide as to how to help you so that you can both make the most of your time. Below are some suggestions on how to use this section.

1. Read it all the way through. It gives you a unique perspective on the grammar at work behind the patterns and characters used in the questions and answers.

2. Personalize it. Take some time to personalize the questions and answers in this part with your own personal details. If someone asks you one of these questions, it is important for you to be able to come up with a suitable personal response. Write out your answers or your likely answers to each of the questions and keep that list handy.

3. Chat. Whether you are face to face or texting, communicating with real people is still the best way to learn a language. You need to

use the questions and answers in this part as often as you can. You don't need to be perfect. In fact, you'll have to make mistakes in order to learn languages. No one, native speaker or foreigner, young or old, has ever learned Mandarin without going through the same things that you are going through right now. If you have a language partner, let the person know that you are focusing on these questions and answers and give the person a copy of them so he or she can help you. You will be able to make the most of your time if both of you are using these questions and answers in your conversations.

Chapter 8: Basic Greetings

Saying "hello" is the first step to start a conversation. We believe that the first word you are taught in class or textbook regarding greetings is 你好(nǐ hǎo). Are you saying 你好(nǐ hǎo) to greet just about anyone you encounter? There is actually a variety of different ways to say "hello" in Chinese. 你好(nǐ hǎo) is often used to greet strangers, and is not used by native Chinese on daily basis. Now, let's learn some typical ones.

吃了吗（chī le ma）?

Have you eaten?

你胖了（nǐ pàng le）!

You're getting fat.

You may find the first sentence strange. Why are people asking me about my meals? Will they invite me for a meal? In actuality, this is just a way to show that the speaker cares about you. Having meals on time is really important in traditional Chinese culture; therefore, many people often start the conversation with this sentence.

You may find the third sentence rude. The literal translation is rude indeed. How can you just say that to my face? But actually, the speaker means that you are eating well, sleeping well, working well... that everything is going well around you, that you look fabulous.

You can use these two greetings with your friends, relatives, or other people you already know well. If you still use 你好(nǐ hǎo) to greet these people, it may be too distant and polite.

Formal greetings in Chinese are really the same as greetings in English. The difference may only the word order. For example:

早（zǎo）！

Morning!

早上好（zǎo shàng hǎo）！

Good morning!

下午好（xià wǔ hǎo）！

Good afternoon!

晚上好（wǎn shàng hǎo）！

Good evening!

晚安（wǎn ān）！

Good night!

好久不见（hǎo jiǔ bú jiàn）！

Long time no see!

你好吗（nǐ hǎo ma）？

How are you?

很高兴认识你（hěn gāo xìng rèn shí nǐ）。

Nice to meet you.

很高兴见到你（hěn gāo xìng jiàn dào nǐ）。

Glad to see you.

代我向你父母问好（dài wǒ xiàng nǐ fù mǔ wèn hǎo）。

Please send my regards to your parents.

再见（zài jiàn）！

Goodbye!

一路顺风（yí lù shùn fēng）！

Have a nice trip!

Chinese people like to use informal greetings in cases where they don't need to use formal greetings. Therefore, as a language learner, we're supposed to greet someone in a Chinese way when speaking Chinese. Here are some more informal Chinese informal:

嘿（hèi）！

Hey!

哈喽（hā lou）！

Hello!

干啥去（gàn shá qù）？

Where are you going?

忙啥呢（máng shá ne）？

What are you busy with?

最近咋样（zuì jìn zǎ yàng）？/ 近来如何（jìn lái rú hé）？

How's everything going lately?

家里还好吧（jiā lǐ hái hǎo ba）？

Is your family well?

出去呀（chū qù ya）？

Going out?

回来了（huí lái le）？

You're back?

Through English translations, you may feel these are nothing special. But we assure you, if you use these sentences to greet your Chinese friends or colleagues (don't use these sentences to greet your supervisors or boss) instead of 你好（nǐ hǎo）, they will be quite happy.

Now you're ready to greet people. Happy chatting.

Chapter 9: Introducing Yourself

We strongly recommend you choose a Chinese name, just as many Chinese people choose an English name. This action will directly shorten the distance between you and your listener.

Chinese naming conventions are quite different from what we know in the west. First names are created rather than picked from a list or passed down. A typical first name is made up of two characters, which is pronounced as two syllables, and they tend to carry some meaning. This is similar to native American naming conventions. There are thousands of characters to choose from, so first names tend to be unique. However, due to China's great population, many people have same names (not only same first name, but also last name).

There is no real list of most common Chinese first names, but last names are a different story. The Chinese present themselves with their last names first. There really aren't all that many different last names in China – about 100 or so are common. Here is a list of the top 10:

李（lǐ）
王（wáng）
张（zhāng）
刘（liú）

陈（chén）
杨（yáng）
赵（zhào）
黄（huáng）
周（zhōu）
吴（wú）

There are several ways to ask someone's name in Chinese, but we'll be taking a look at the most common ones. Let's check out the question first.

你叫什么名字（nǐ jiào shén me míng zi）？

What is your name?

您贵姓（nín guì xìng）？

May I have your family name please?

From the English translations, we can see that the first question is quite casual while the second is quite formal. Therefore, you will hear people ask the first question in everyday life, and the second in very formal occasions. So, what are the answers? Let's use a typical Chinese name - 李小龙（lǐ xiǎo lóng）in our examples.

The answer to the first question:

我叫李小龙（wǒ jiào lǐ xiǎo lóng）。

I'm Li Xiaolong./My name is Li Xiaolong.

The answer to the second question:

免贵姓李（miǎn guì xìng lǐ）。

Please just call me Li.

After knowing your name, another question follows, and that is to ask where you are from:

你是哪国人（nǐ shì nǎ guó rén）？ or 你从哪里来（nǐ cóng nǎ lǐ lái）？

Here we are literally asking "you are which country person?" or "You from where come?" Although the literal translation sounds awkard in English, it is easy to see how the words match up.

Then, how do you say your nationality?

Pattern: 我是（wǒ shì）+ country name + 人（rén）

For example:

我是美国人（wǒ shì měi guó rén）。

I'm American.

我是德国人（wǒ shì dé guó rén）。

I'm German.

我是意大利人（wǒ shì yì dà lì rén）。

I'm Italian.

我是日本人（wǒ shì rì běn rén）。

I'm Japanese.

And how do you say, "I am from..."?

Pattern: someone + 是（shì）+ 从（cóng）+ country/city/place + 来的（lái de）

For example:

我是从英国来的（wǒ shì cóng yīng guó lái de）。

I'm from England.

她是从北京来的（tā shì cóng běi jīng lái de）。

She's from Beijing.

我朋友是从澳大利亚来的（wǒ péng yǒu shì cóng ào dà lì yà lái de）。

My friend comes from Australia.

Other than questions, here are more things you can introduce about yourself or your family.

How to tell someone "where you do something"?

Pattern: subject + 在（zài）+ place + predicate

For example:

我在北京大学教数学（wǒ zài běi jīng dà xué jiāo shù xué）。

I teach math in Peking University.

她在加拿大工作（tā zài jiā ná dà gōng zuò）。

She works in Canada.

In Chinese word order, the place must come before the predicate. In other words, while in English you can say "I work in China," in

Chinese you must say 我在中国工作（wǒ zài zhōng guó gōng zuò）; it is incorrect to say 我工作在中国（wǒ gōng zuò zài zhōng guó）.

How do you say what someone does for a living?

There are three patterns. The first one is who + 是（shì）+ name of profession. It is used to say someone "is a" teacher, student, doctor, etc. For example:

我姐姐是护士（wǒ jiě jie shì hù shì）。
My older sister is a nurse.
我老公是警察（wǒ lǎo gōng shì jǐng chá）。
My husband is a policeman.

The second one is who + 在（zài）+ place + 工作（gōng zuò）. It is used to say someone "works at/in" a school, hospital, library, etc. For example:

我爸爸在工厂工作（wǒ bà ba zài gōng chǎng gōng zuò）。
My father works in a factory.
你哥哥在阿里巴巴工作吗（nǐ gē ge zài ā lǐ bā bā gōng zuò ma）？
Does your older brother work at Alibaba?

The third one is who + 做（zuò）+ name of profession. It is used to say someone "works as a" doctor, driver, actor, etc. This pattern is often used in sentences where "to work as" follows another verb or adjective. For example:

你想做科学家吗（nǐ xiǎng zuò kē xué jiā ma）？
Do you want to be a scientist?
你想不想做演员（nǐ xiǎng bù xiǎng zuò yǎn yuán）？
Do you want to become an actor?

How to talk about your hobbies?

Pattern: 我的爱好是（wǒ de ài hào shì）... For example:
我的爱好是唱歌（wǒ de ài hào shì chàng gē）。
I like singing./My hobby is to sing.
我的爱好是钓鱼（wǒ de ài hào shì diào yú）。

I like fishing./My hobby is to go fishing.

To help you make a complete introduction, here are two paragraphs you can work on. After mastering the language, you can replace the details with yours.

Simple (you can use this in your daily life):

我叫李小龙。我是中国人。三年前，我在美国教中文。现在我在中国当翻译。我的父亲已经退休了，母亲在中学做老师。我喜欢打篮球和踢足球。

wǒ jiào lǐ xiǎo long. wǒ shì zhōng guó rén. sān nián qián, wǒ zài měi guó jiāo zhōng wén. xiàn zài wǒ zài zhōng guó dāng fān yì. wǒ de fù qīn yǐ jīng tuì xiū le, mǔ qīn zài zhōng xué zuò lǎo shī. wǒ xǐ huān dǎ lán qiú hé tī zú qiú.

I'm Li Xiaolong. I'm from China. Three years ago, I taught Chinese in America. Now, I work as a translator in China. My father has retired from work, and my mother works at a middle school. I like play basketball and football.

Hard (you can use this in a job interview):

下午好！我的名字是李小龙。今天有机会进行自我介绍深感荣幸。我乐意回答你们所提出来的任何问题。我希望我今天能表现的非常出色。我今年三十岁，出生在北京。我有很多兴趣爱好，如唱歌、跳舞、画画等。我目前是一家外贸公司的部门经理。我觉得自己是个工作勤奋、负责、能干，而且外向的人。依我的资格和经验，我觉得我对所从事的每一个项目都很努力、负责、勤勉。我的分析能力和与人相处的技巧，对贵单位必有价值。我希望能获得一份更好的工作，如果机会来临，我会抓住。我的工作经验使我适合这份工作。并且我相信我能成功。

xià wǔ hǎo! wǒ de míng zi shì lǐ xiǎo long. jīn tiān yǒu jī huì jìn xíng zì wǒ jiè shào shēn gǎn róng xìng. wǒ lè yì huí dá nǐ men suǒ tí chū lái de rèn hé wèn tí. wǒ xī wàng wǒ jīn tiān néng biǎo xiàn de fēi cháng chū sè. wǒ jīn nián sān shí suì, chū shēng zài běi jīng. wǒ yǒu hěn duō xìng qù ài hào, rú chàng gē, tiào wǔ, huà huà děng. wǒ mù qián shì yì jiā wài mào gōng sī de bù mén jīng lǐ. yī wǒ de zī gé hé jīng yàn, wǒ jué de wǒ duì suǒ cóng shì de měi yí gè xiàng mù dōu hěn nǔ lì, fù zé, qín miǎn. wǒ de fèn xī néng lì hé yǔ rén xiàng chǔ de jì qiǎo, duì guì dān wèi bì yǒu jià zhí. wǒ xī wàng néng huò dé yí fèn gèng hǎo de gōng zuò, rú guǒ jī huì lái lín, wǒ huì zhuā zhù. wǒ de gōng zuò jīng yàn shǐ wǒ shì hé zhè fèn gōng zuò. bìng qiě wǒ xiàng xìn wǒ néng chéng gōng. wǒ jué dé zì jǐ shì gè gōng zuò qín fèn, fù zé, néng gàn, ér qiě wài xiàng de rén.

Good afternoon, my name is Li Xiaolong. It is really a great honor to have this opportunity to introduce myself. I would like to answer whatever questions you may raise, and I hope I can make a good impression today. I'm thirty years old, born in Beijing. I currently work as a department manager in a trading company. I'm hard-working, responsible, capable, and outgoing. I have lots of interests, such as singing, dancing, drawing, and so on. With my qualifications and experience, I feel I am capable of managing projects I undertake with responsibility and diligence. Your organization could benefit from my analytical and interpersonal skills. I am hoping to get an offer of a better position. If an opportunity knocks, I will take it. My work experience should qualify me for this particular job. I am sure I will be successful.

At the end of this chapter, we will introduce you to Chinese zodaics, including 鼠（shǔ）, 牛（niú）, 虎（hǔ）, 兔（tù）, 龙（lóng）, 蛇（shé）, 马（mǎ）, 羊（yáng）, 猴（hóu）, 鸡（jī）, 狗（gǒu）, and 猪（zhū）. The origin of Chinese zodaics, in fact, has many different versions. If you can use Chinese zodaic to introduce yourself, you listener will be impressed.

Long, long ago, there was no concept of time. There were no clocks or calendars. People wanted to mark the passing of time but didn't know how. Therefore, they sought advice from the Emperor, known for his wisdom in such matters. He pondered for a considerable time before deigning to offer his learned advice: "Because animals and humans have a close affinity and the names of animals are easily remembered, they should be used to symbolize time. Henceforth, a river race shall be held to determine those animals best suited to signify time".

Thereupon the event was held. All manner of beasts attended. The cat and the mouse, who were good friends, discussed the best manner in which to cross, as neither could swim. They decided to ask the ox to aid them. The ox, being a sincere and kindhearted soul, agreed to carry them across. The race began and the ox, who was by far the best swimmer, emerged in the lead. As they neared the finish line, the cat proudly rose and declared the three of them to be the first to cross the line. However, the mouse, a cunning and selfish soul, secretly desired to cross the line first. He caught the cat unaware, pushed him into the water., and jumped behind the ox's ear.

The ox, unaware of the commotion, swam on to the finish line. Just as he reached the shore, the mouse leaped forward and ran to victory, quickly followed by the ox, the tiger, the rabbit, the dragon, the snake, the horse, the sheep, the monkey, the rooster, the dog, and the pig.

The exhausted cat finally scrambled to shore, but the race was already over. The cat was extremely angry at the mouse, and every time they met, the cat would try to bite him. He then told of the mouse's crime to all his progeny, beginning a feud between the two animals which continues to this very day.

The mouse, knowing full-well his sin, skulked away in guilt and spent the rest of his days hiding in dark, sullen places.

The rabbit, who could not swim, made the crossing by leaping across the other animal's heads. He acquired his peculiarly shaped mouth because he ran too fast, and after crossing the finish line, ran into a tree.

The dragon, who should have been placed higher in the ranking, had been busy in the heavens creating thunder and lightning. He absent-mindedly made the thunder too loud, which caused minor deafness. As a consequence, he did not hear the start of the race and had to come from behind to acquire fifth place.

The snake, in order to defeat the horse, scared him and dashed in front. Unfortunately for his, he ran too fast, causing his four legs to break off, leaving him in his present legless state.

The sheep, monkey, and rooster had agreed to make the crossing together. They did so by putting the sheep on the shoulders of the monkey, who in turn sat upon the back of the rooster. As they were crossing, the sheep who was a sort of lookout saw the dog who was naughtily bathing in the river and scolded him severely. The dog continued the race and finished next to last but didn't really care. The sheep ended up overstraining his eyes and permanently damaged his vision. The monkey, who sat far too long, acquired a permanently red posterior. The rooster, who had been supporting the group, lost two of his original four legs as they were crushed.

The pig finished last as he decided to finish eating before crossing the river. When he finally made it across, he entreated the Emperor for more food. His gluttony caused him to become the laughing stock of all those present.

This is a story about how the system of Chinese zodaics was created. In China, each year is denoted by one of twelve different animals. Your zodaic is supposed to be an indicator of your personality.

In addition, more and more Chinese people, especially the younger generation, have started to believe in astrology. During your self-introduction, you can also talk about that. Here are the expressions of constellations in Chinese.

白羊座（bái yáng zuò）Aries

金牛座（jīn niú zuò）Taurus

双子座（shuāng zǐ zuò）Gemini

巨蟹座（jù xiè zuò）Cancer

狮子座（shī zi zuò）Leo

处女座（chù nǚ zuò）Virgo

天平座（tiān píng zuò）Libra

天蝎座（tiān xiē zuò）Scorpio

射手座（shè shǒu zuò）Sagittarius
摩羯座（mó jié zuò）Capricorn
水瓶座（shuǐ píng zuò）Aquarius
双鱼座（shuāng yú zuò）Pisces

Chapter 10: Formulating Questions and Dialogue:

As we learned in Chapter 7, there are five different kind of questions: the yes or no question, the question using an interrogative pronoun, the affirmative and negative question, the alternative question, and the rhetorical question. Now, let's learn how to form these questions.

Yes or no questions are formed by adding the interrogative particle 吗（ma）or 吧（ba）at the end of a declarative sentence. For example:

她是张教授（tā shì zhāng jiào shòu）。

She's Professor Zhang.

她是张教授吗（tā shì zhāng jiào shòu ma）？

Is she Professor Zhang?

他明天回来（tā míng tiān huí lai）。

He will be back tomorrow.

他明天回来吧（tā míng tiān huí lai ba）？

Will he be back tomorrow?

Questions using interrogative pronouns are made from declarative sentences by replacing the enquired information with the interrogative pronoun. What should be specially noted is that the word order of such a question is exactly the same as that of the declarative sentence, i.e. the question is formed by putting the interrogative pronoun in the position where the answer is expected, not at the beginning. For example:

那是我的外套（nà shì wǒ de wài tào）。
That is my coat.

那是谁的外套（nà shì shuí de wài tào）?
Whose coat is that?

餐馆在路的左侧（cān guǎn zài lù de zuǒ cè）。
The restaurant is on the left side of the road.

餐馆在哪里（cān guǎn zài nǎ lǐ）?
Where is the restaurant?

For more interrogative pronouns, you can review our previous chapters.

好吗/行吗/可以吗/对吗（hǎo ma/xíng ma/kě yǐ ma/duì ma）can be used at the end of declarative sentence to form affirmative and negative questions. For example:

我们听听音乐，好吗（wǒ men tīng tīng yīn yuè, hǎo ma）?
Let's listen to the music, shall we?

这个单词这么念，对吗（zhè gè dān cí zhè me niàn, duì ma）?
This word is pronounced like this, right?

Another way to form affirmative and negative questions is by putting affirmative and negative forms of the predicate together. For example:

好不好（hǎo bú hǎo）

行不行（xíng bù xíng）

能不能（néng bù néng）

对不对（duì bú duì）

是不是（shì bú shì）

你能不能帮帮我（nǐ néng bù néng bāng bāng wǒ）?

Can you help me or not?

我是不是在做梦（wǒ shì bú shì zài zuò mèng）？

Am I dreaming or not?

The alternative question is a question in which several alternatives are paralleled by the conjunction 还是（hái shì）for the answerer to choose. The basic patterns are:

是（shì）......还是（hái shì）......?

Sometimes the first 是（shì）can be ommited. For example:

她是美国人还是法国人（tā shì měi guó rén hái shì fǎ guó rén）？

Is she American or a French?

他高还是你高（tā gāo hái shì nǐ gāo）？

Which one of you is taller? You or him?

Rhetorical questions are often formed by two major patterns:

Using 哪儿......啊 to refute a certain case that is not in keeping with the fact and using 不是......吗 to express the meaning of certainty. For example:

我哪儿知道啊（wǒ nǎr zhī dào a）？

I don't really know.

你哪儿不知道啊（nǐ nǎr bù zhī dào ā）？

How can you not know?

你不是去过我家吗（nǐ bú shì qù guò wǒ jiā ma）？

You have been to my house, haven't you?

不是你去过我家吗（bú shì nǐ qù guò wǒ jiā ma）？

Wern't you the one that was at my house.

Before we more on, let's learn to make the question more polite.

Pattern: 请问 (qǐng wèn) + question

A question prefaced with 请问 (qǐng wèn) is much more polite than one that is not. The English translation of 请问 (qǐng wèn) depends on the context.

Example:

请问这个多少钱 (qǐng wèn zhè gè duō shǎo qián)？

May I ask how much this is?

请问书店在哪里 (qǐng wèn shū diàn zài nǎ lǐ)？

Could you please tell me where the bookstore is?

Buying and Ordering

How do I ask "Do you have any..."?

Pattern: 有没有（yǒu méi yǒu）+ the thing you are looking for

This pattern is used for asking if someone has something, whether or not something is available, or even whether or not something exists.

Examples:

有没有塑料袋（yǒu méi yǒu sù liào dài）？

 Do you have any plastic bags?

有没有现金（yǒu méi yǒu xiàn jīn）？

Do you have any cash?

How do I ask "How much do/does... cost"?

Pattern: the thing you are interested in + 多少钱（duō shǎo qián）

Examples:

纪念品多少钱（jì niàn pǐn duō shǎo qián）？

How much do souvenirs cost?

火车票多少钱（huǒ chē piào duō shǎo qián）？

How much does the train ticket cost?

How do I ask to buy something of a certain cost?

This pattern is complicated, but worth learning if you need to buy items denominated by price:

我要（wǒ yào）+ number of items + measure word + cost + 的（de）+ item

For example:

我要两个十块钱的杯子（wǒ yào liǎng gè shí kuài qián de bēi zi）。

I want two 10 *yuan* cups.

我要买六支三元的笔（wǒ yào mǎi liù zhī sān yuán de bǐ）。

I want to buy six 3 *yuan* pens.

How do I say "I'm a bit hungry（thirsty, sleepy, etc.）"?

Pattern: subject + 有点（yǒu diǎn）+ adjective

For example:

我有点饿（wǒ yǒu diǎn è）。

I'm a bit hungry.

我有点渴（wǒ yǒu diǎn kě）。

I'm a bit thirsty.

这里有点冷（zhè lǐ yǒu diǎn lěng）。

It's a little cold here.

How do I say "a sweet one（a big one, a shiny one, etc.）"?

Pattern: adjective + 的（de）

我要那个大的（wǒ yào nà gè dà de）。

I want that big one.

他喜欢咸的（tā xǐ huān xián de）。

He likes the salty kind.

你想吃甜的吗（nǐ xiǎng chī tián de ma）?

Do you want to have something sweet?

How do I ask an either/or question?

Pattern: A + 还是（hái shì）+ B

For example:

For adjectives:

这是酸的还是辣的（zhè shì suān de hái shì là de）?

Is this sour or hot?

你要大的还是小的（nǐ yào dà de hái shì xiǎo de）?

Do you want a big one or a small one?

For nouns:

你想喝可乐还是啤酒（nǐ xiǎng hē kě lè hái shì pí jiǔ）?

Do you want to have a bottle coke or some beer?

How can I compare two things?

Pattern: A + 比（bǐ）+ B + adjective

For example:

这件比那件贵（zhè jiàn bǐ nà jiàn guì）。

This one is more expensive than that one.

这个比那个好吃 (zhè gè bǐ nà gè hǎo chī)。

This thing tastes better than that.

Another way to compare is by using 一点（yì diǎn）. Pattern: adjective + 一点（yì diǎn）

For example:

这件外套便宜一点（zhè jiàn wài tào pián yi yì diǎn）。

This coat is a little cheaper.

这家店的价格高一点（zhè jiā diàn de jià gé gāo yì diǎn）。

The price of this store is a little higher.

How do I place an order at a restaurant or store?

Pattern: subject + 要（yào）+ amount + measure word + item

For example:

我要两碗面（wǒ yào liǎng wǎn miàn）。

I'll have two bowls of noodles.

我要这件外套（wǒ yào zhè jiàn wài tào）。

I want this coat.

How do I say what color of something I want?

Pattern: color + 的（de）or color + 色（sè）+ 的（de）

Example:

我要那个红的（wǒ yào nà gè hóng de）。

I want that red one.

我想买那个白色的（wǒ xiǎng mǎi nà gè bái sè de）。

I want to buy that white colored one.

Can you buy or order things in Chinese now? If you are still wondering how, let's read these dialogues together!

Dialogue 1:

A: 你要买什么（nǐ yào mǎi shén me）？

What would you like to buy?

B: 我想看看那件 T 恤（wǒ xiǎng kàn kan nà jiàn T xù）。

I would like to look at that T-shirt.

A: 你要什么颜色（nǐ yào shén me yán sè）？

What color do you want?

B: 我要那个白的（wǒ yào nà gè bái de）。

I want that white one.

A: 给你这件（gěi nǐ zhè jiàn）。

Please take a look at this one.

B: 这件太小了。有大号的吗（zhè jiàn tài xiǎo le. yǒu dà hào de ma）？

This one is too small, do you have a bigger size?

A: 对不起，白色没有大号的了，你试试这件蓝色的吧（duì bù qǐ, bái sè méi yǒu dà hào de le, nǐ shì shi zhè jiàn lán sè de ba）。

Sorry, we don't have a bigger size of the white one. Please try this blue one.

B: 很漂亮，我买了。多少钱（hěn piào liang, wǒ mǎi le. duō shǎo qián）？

It's beautiful. I'll take it. How much?

A: 200 块（liǎng bǎi kuài）。

200 *yuan.*

Dialogue 2:

A: 你饿了吗（nǐ è le ma）？

Are you hungry?

B: 有点儿（yǒu diǎn er）。

A little.

A: 我们出去吃饭吧（wǒ men chū qù chī fàn ba）。

Let's go out to eat.

A: 请给我菜单，我要点菜（qǐng gěi wǒ cài dān, wǒ yào diǎn cài）。

Please give me a menu. I'd like to order.

C: 您想吃点什么（nín xiǎng chī diǎn shén me）？

What would you like to eat?

A: 你有什么好建议（nǐ yǒu shén me hǎo jiàn yì）？

Any good suggestion?

C: 这里的清蒸鱼很好，来两份试试吧（zhè lǐ de qīng zhēng yú hěn hǎo, lái liǎng fèn shì shi ba）。

Our steamed fish is very good. Would you lke to have a try?

A: 好，那就来两盘（hǎo, nà jiù lái liǎng pán）。

Sure. Two dishes of steamed fish then.

C: 好的。喝点什么（hǎo de. hē diǎn shén me）？

Ok. What would you like to drink?

A: 我要一瓶啤酒（wǒ yào yì píng pí jiǔ）。

I would like to have a bottle of beer.

B: 一杯红酒（yì bēi hóng jiǔ）。

A glass of wine.

C: 请等一下，菜马上就来（qǐng děng yí xià, cài mǎ shàng jiù lái）。

Please wait a moment. The dishes will be served soon.

B: 买单（mǎi dān）。

Check please.

C: 好的。一共九十五块。您给我一百块，找您三块零钱（hǎo de. yí gòng jiǔ shí wǔ kuài. nín gěi wǒ yì bǎi kuài, zhǎo nín sān kuài líng qián）。

Ok. The total is 97 *yuan*. You gave me 100 *yuan*. Here it is your change, 3 *yuan*.

B: 请给我发票（qǐng gěi wǒ fā piào）。

May I have a receipt?

C: 没问题。欢迎下次光临（méi wèn tí. huān yíng xià cì guāng lín）。

No problem. Please come again soon.

At Work/School/College

How do I ask "What does... mean"?

Pattern: unfamiliar word + 是（shì）+ 什么意思（shén me yì sī）

Examples:

这句话是什么意思 (zhè jù huà shì shén me yì sī)？

What does this sentence mean?

How do I ask how to do something?

Pattern: subject + 怎么（zěn me）+ verb

For example:

传真机怎么用（chuán zhēn jī zěn me yòng）？

How do I use the fax machine?

这道题怎么做（zhè dào tí zěn me zuò）？

How do I solve this question?

How do I say I want to do something myself?

The sentence pattern is often used when emphasizing that one can or will do something themselves and doesn't need assistance.

Pattern: pronoun + 自己（zì jǐ）+ verb

For example:

我自己来（wǒ zì jǐ lái）。

I'll do it myself.

我自己去（wǒ zì jǐ qù）。

I can go there myself.

他自己没问题（tā zì jǐ méi wèn tí）。

He can do that by himself.

How do I say "I want to do something"?

Pattern: subject + 想（xiǎng）+ verb + object

For example:

我想请个假（wǒ xiǎng qǐng gè jià）。
I want to take a day off.
你想休息一下吗（nǐ xiǎng xiū xī yī xià ma）？
Do you want to take a break?
How do I ask "Do you have..."?
Chinese often uses a topic-comment sentence pattern during work, and this pattern can be used to ask the "Do you have..." question.
Pattern: topic + 有没有（yǒu méi yǒu）
For example:
工作服有没有（gōng zuò fú yǒu méi yǒu）？
Do you have work clothes?
安全帽有没有（ān quán mào yǒu méi yǒu）？
Do you have a safety helmet?
How do I politely ask someone to do something for me?
Pattern: 请（qǐng）+ 你（nǐ）+ 帮（bāng）+ who + do what
For example:
请帮我开门（qǐng bāng wǒ kāi mén）。
Please open the door for me
请你帮我修理打印机（qǐng nǐ bāng wǒ xiū lǐ dǎ yìn jī）。
Please fix the printer for me.
请你帮我向老师请假（qǐng nǐ bāng wǒ xiàng lǎo shī qǐng jià）。
Please help me ask for leave from the teacher
How do I say "wait a minute (a moment, a bit, etc.)"
Pattern: verb + 一下（yí xià）
For example:
等一下（děng yí xià）wait a minute
看一下（kàn yí xià）look for a moment
让一下（ràng yí xià）move a bit
How can I politely make a request?
Pattern: 麻烦（má fan）+ 你/您（nǐ/nín）+ request
For example:

麻烦你给我那个本子（má fan nǐ gěi wǒ nà gè běn zi）。
Can I trouble you to give me that notebook?

麻烦你帮我写份报告（má fan nǐ bāng wǒ xiě fèn bào gào）。
Can I trouble you to write me a report?

麻烦您到我公司来一趟（má fan nín dào wǒ gōng sī lái yí tàng）。
Can I trouble you to come over to our company?

How do I state a time?

For hours, use this pattern: number + 点（diǎn）

Adding 钟（zhōng）after 点（diǎn）is optional in this pattern. For example:

三点（sān diǎn）three o'clock

四点钟（sì diǎn zhōng）four o'clock

For minutes, use the pattern: number + 分（fēn）

For example:

三点十分（sān diǎn shí fēn）2:10

四点五十三分（sì diǎn wǔ shí sān fēn）4:53

How do I say "I am doing something"?

Pattern: 在（zài）+ verb

For example:

我在打电话（wǒ zài dǎ diàn huà）。
I'm on the phone.

他在听音乐（tā zài tīng yīn yuè）。
He's listening to music.

What is the word order for using 已经（yǐ jīng）in a sentence?

Pattern: subject + 已经（yǐ jīng）+ predicate

For example:

他已经工作两年（tā yǐ jīng gōng zuò liǎng nián）。
He has been working for two years already.

你已经在厕所很久（nǐ yǐ jīng zài cè suǒ hěn jiǔ）。
You've already been in the bathroom a long time!

Notice that, unlike "already" in English, 已经（yǐ jīng）can't be placed at the end of a sentence.

How do I make a suggestion?

One pattern for making suggestions is: noun phrase/sentence + 怎么样（zěn me yàng）

For example:

先写报告怎么样（xiān xiě bào gào zěn me yàng）?

How about we write the report first?

去打篮球怎么样（qù dǎ lán qiú zěn me yàng）?

What about playing basketball?

Another way to make a suggestion is with the particle 吧 (ba).

For example:

我们走吧（wǒ men zǒu ba）。

Let's leave.

我们去开会吧（wǒ men qù kāi huì ba）。

Let's go to the meeting.

How do I say "Did you do something or not"?

Pattern: subject + 有没有（yǒu méi yǒu）+ verb + object

For example:

你有没有带工作证（nǐ yǒu méi yǒu dài gōng zuò zhèng）?

Did you bring your work card or not?

你有没有关上教室的窗户（nǐ yǒu méi yǒu guān shàng jiào shì de chuāng hu）?

Did you close the window of the classroom?

The answer to this question is really easy, just simply repeat the verb with 了（le）at the end for a positive answer; or say 没（méi）at first and then repeat the verb for a negative answer.

How do I say "before/after doing something..."?

Pattern: verb + noun + 以后/以前（yǐ hòu/yǐ qián）

放学以后我们去打篮球吧（fàng xué yǐ hòu wǒ men qù dǎ lán qiú ba）?

Let's play basketball after school.

上班之前我去了趟医院（shàng bān zhī qián wǒ qù le tàng yī yuàn）。

I went the hospital before going to work.

What is the sentence pattern for making an appointment including time and place?

Pattern: subject + time + place + predicate

For example:

我们三点在广场见（wǒ men sān diǎn zài guǎng chǎng jiàn）。

Let's meet at the plaza at three.

我一会儿去机场接你（wǒ yì huìr qù jī chǎng jiē nǐ）。

I'll pick you at the airport later.

Here are more sentences you may find useful when you speak Chinese in real life:

对不起，我迟到了（duì bù qǐ, wǒ chí dào le）。

Sorry, I'm late.

这个字/词怎么读（zhè gè zì/cí zěn me dú）?

How do you pronounce this character/word?

请您再说一遍（qǐng nín zài shuō yí biàn）。

Please say it again.

请您慢一点（qǐng nín màn yì diǎn）。

Please speak a little slowly.

这是我的名片（zhè shì wǒ de míng piàn）。

Here's my business card.

我来这里开会（wǒ lái zhè lǐ kāi huì）。

I'm here for a meeting.

我们可以定个见面时间吗（wǒ men kě yǐ dìng ge jiàn miàn shí jiān ma）?

May I make an appointment?

Travelling

China has an excellent rail network which links all the major cities and smaller towns, as well as an extensive bus system for long-distance travel. Most big cities have their own underground subway systems as well as taxis and public buses. Although you can rent a car in many cities, you can usually only drive within the city limits, and may have to hire a driver if you wish to travel farther around this vast country.

How do I ask "Where can I..."

Pattern: 哪里（nǎ lǐ）+ 可以（kě yǐ）+ verb + object

For example:

哪里可以吃饭（nǎ lǐ kě yǐ chī fàn）？

Where can we get something to eat?

哪里可以打车（nǎ lǐ kě yǐ dǎ chē）？

Where can I take a taxi?

How do I state a destination?

Pattern: 到（dào）+ place

For example:

到火车站（dào huǒ chē zhàn）。

To the train station.

到机场（dào jī chǎng）。

To the airport.

How do I say "the car, the train, or whatever to somewhere"?

Pattern: 到（dào）+ destination + possessive

到上海的火车在哪里（dào shàng hǎi de huǒ chē zài nǎ lǐ）？

Where is the train to Shanghai?

出租车不到喜来登酒店吗（chū zū chē bú dào xǐ lái dēng jiǔ diàn ma）？

Is this cab to Sheraton Hotel?

How do I ask "Where is..."?

Pattern: place + 在哪里（zài nǎ lǐ）

For example:

飞机场在哪里（fēi jī chǎng zài nǎ lǐ）？
Where is the airport?

厕所在哪里（cè suǒ zài nǎ lǐ）？
Where is the bathroom?

What is the answer to "Where is..."?

Pattern: destination + 在（zài）+ direction or direction + 有（yǒu）+ place

For example:

火车站在前面（huǒ chē zhàn zài qián miàn）。
The train station is ahead.

那边有公园（nà biān yǒu gōng yuán）。
There is park over there.

How do I answer "how long" questions?

Below are sample answer patterns for "how long" questions like

你已经在中国多久（nǐ yǐ jīng zài zhōng guó duō jiǔ）？
How long have you been in China?

一分钟（yì fēn zhōng）。
One minute.

For this pattern, you must add 钟（zhōng）

一个小时（yí gè xiǎo shí）。
One hour.

一天（yì tiān）。
A day.

一个星期（yí gè xīng qī）。
A week.

一个月（yí gè yuè）。
A month.

一年（yì nián）。
One year.

Note which of the above phrases require a measure word and which do not.

How do I say that doing something is (not) permitted somewhere?

Pattern: place + 可以/不可以（kě yǐ/bù kě yǐ）+ action

For example:

这里可以停车（zhè lǐ kě yǐ tíng chē）。

It's permitted to stop the vehicle here.

在博物馆不可以吸烟（zài bó wù guǎn bù kě yǐ xī yān）。

You are not allowed to smoke in the museum.

Notice in Chinese word order that the place comes first.

Here are more sentences you may find useful when you speak Chinese in real life:

书店怎么去（shū diàn zěn me qù）？

How do I get to the bookstone?

我迷路了（wǒ mí lù le）。

I'm lost.

附近有厕所吗（fù jìn yǒu cè suǒ ma）？

Is there a toilet nearby?

最近的酒店有多远（zuì jìn de jiǔ diàn yǒu duō yuǎn）？

How far is the nearest hotel?

这是去公园的路吗（zhè shì qù gōng yuán de lù ma）？

Is this the road to the park?

我上车之前要检票吗（wǒ shàng chē zhī qián yào jiǎn piào ma）？

Do I stamp the ticket before boarding?

从哪个站台离开（cóng nǎ gè zhàn tái lí kāi）？

Which platform does it leave from?

需要多长时间（xū yào duō cháng shí jiān）？

How long does it take?

我在哪能找到出租车（wǒ zài nǎ néng zhǎo dào chū zū chē）？

Where can I get a taxi?

你能把我放在这里吗（nǐ néng bǎ wǒ fàng zài zhè lǐ ma）？

Can you drop me here?

我能要一个收据吗（wǒ néng yào yí gè shōu jù ma）？
May I have a receipt?
我去哪办理登记手续（wǒ qù nǎ bàn lǐ dēng jì shǒu xù）？
Where do I check in?
我需要办理一件行李托运（wǒ xū yào bàn lǐ yí jiàn xíng li tuō yùn）。
I'm checking in one suitcase.
我什么时候登机（wǒ shén me shí hòu dēng jī）？
What time do I board?
我找不到我的行李（wǒ zhǎo bú dào wǒ de xíng li）。
I can't find my luggage.

Other things you may want to know

Unlike in America, most Chinese doctors are based in hopitals; you will need to make an appointment to see one. Many pharmacies stock Western medicines as well as traditional Chinese remedies and can treat you for most minor health problems. It is a good idea to familiarize yourself with a few basic phrases for use in an emergency or in case you need to visit a pharmacy or doctor.

What is the sentence pattern for saying some part of my body hurts?

Pattern: 我（wǒ） + part of body + problem
For example:
我头疼（wǒ tóu téng）。
I have a headache.
我背酸（wǒ bèi suān）。
I have a sore back.
我眼睛不舒服（wǒ yǎn jīng bù shū fú）。
My eyes are uncomfortable.
我耳朵很痒（wǒ ěr duǒ hěn yǎng）。
My ear is itchy.
Other useful sentences:
我有健康保险（wǒ yǒu jiàn kāng bǎo xiǎn）。

I have health insurance.

我需要看牙医（wǒ xū yào kàn yá yī）。
I need a dentist.

治咳嗽该吃什么药（zhì ké sòu gāi chī shén me yào）?
What can I take for coughs?

有副作用吗（yǒu fù zuò yòng ma）?
Are there side effects?

我需要一个处方吗（wǒ xū yào yí gè chù fāng ma）?
Do I need a prescription?

In the event of an emergency, you should dial one of the following emergency numbers: 110 for the police, 119 for the fire department, and 120 for an ambulance. If you are the victim of a crime or you've lost your passport and money, you should report the incident to the police, although it may be best to seek advice first from your local embassy or consulate staff. Here are some useful sentences:

救命（jiù mìng）!
Help!

放手（fàng shǒu）!
Let go.

打电话报警（dǎ diàn huà bào jǐng）!
Call the police!

有人受伤了，请快来（yǒu rén shòu shāng le, qǐng kuài lái）!
Someone's injured, please come quickly!

我孩子丢了（wǒ hái zi diū le）。
My child is missing.

我被打劫了（wǒ bèi dǎ jié le）。
I've been robbed.

Common conversation starters:

你家里有几口人（nǐ jiā lǐ yǒu jǐ kǒu rén）?
How many people are there in your family?

你有没有兄弟姐妹（nǐ yǒu méi yǒu xiōng dì jiě mèi）?
Do you have any brothers or sisters?

你结婚了吗（nǐ jié hūn le ma）？
Are you married?

你有孩子吗（nǐ yǒu hái zi ma）？
Do you have any children?

你的老家在哪里（nǐ de lǎo jiā zài nǎ lǐ）？
Where is your hometown?

你一个月多少钱（nǐ yí gè yuè duō shǎo qián）？
How much do you make a month?

你的工资多少钱（nǐ de gōng zī duō shǎo qián）？
What is your salary?

你想家吗（nǐ xiǎng jiā ma）？
Do you miss your home?

你在这里习惯吗（nǐ zài zhè lǐ xí guàn ma）？
Are you accustomed to life here?

你觉得这里怎么样（nǐ jué de zhè lǐ zěn me yàng）？
What do you think about here?

APPENDIX: VOCABULARY
Glossary of Nouns

姓（xìng）surname
名（míng）first name
姓名（xìng míng）full name
爸爸（bà ba）dad
父亲（fù qin）father
妈妈（mā ma）mom
母亲（mǔ qin）mother
叔叔（shū shu）uncle
阿姨（ā yí）aunt
爷爷（yé ye）grandfather (father's dad)
奶奶（nǎi nai）grandmother (father's mom)
外公（wài gōng）grandfather (mother's dad)
外婆（wài pó）grandmother (mother's mom)
女儿（nǚ er）daughter
儿子（ér zi）son
先生（xiān shēng）Mr., sir

女士（nǚ shì）Madam, Miss., Ms.
夫人（fū rén）Ms.
太太（tài tài）Ms.
哥哥（gē ge）older brother
姐姐（jiě jie）order sister
弟弟（dì di）younger brother
妹妹（mèi mei）younger sister
男孩（nán hái）boy
女孩（nǚ hái）girl
朋友（péng yǒu）friend
室友（shì yǒu）roommate
同学（tóng xué）classmate
伙伴（huǒ bàn）companion
恋人（liàn rén）lover
伴侣（bàn lǚ）mate, partner
夫妻（fū qī）husband and wife
丈夫（zhàng fu）husband
老公（lǎo gōng）husband
妻子（qī zǐ）wife
老婆（lǎo pó）wife
医生（yī shēng）doctor
经理（jīng lǐ）manager
演员（yǎn yuán）actor, actress
歌手（gē shǒu）singer
记者（jì zhě）journalist
工程师（gōng chéng shī）engineer
顾问（gù wèn）consultant
老师（lǎo shī）teacher
警察（jǐng chá）police officer
工人（gōng rén）worker

司机（sī jī）driver
公务员（gōng wù yuán）government official
律师（lǜ shī）lawyer
科学家（kē xué jiā）scientist
服务员（fú wù yuán）waiter, waitress
接待员（jiē dài yuán）receptionist
厨师（chú shī）chef
翻译（fān yì）translator
作家（zuò jiā）writer
艺术家（yì shù jiā）artist
销售员（xiāo shòu yuán）salesperson
商人（shāng rén）businessman, businesswoman
企业家（qǐ yè jiā）enterpreneur
学生（xué shēng）student
秘书（mì shū）secretary
护士（hù shì）nurse
消防员（xiāo fáng yuán）firefighter
飞行员（fēi háng yuán）pilot
空乘（kōng chéng）flight attendant
教授（jiāo shòu）professor
校长（xiào zhǎng）headmaster
志愿者（zhì yuàn zhě）volunteer
军人（jūn rén）armyman
文化（wén huà）culture
语言（yǔ yán）language
文学（wén xué）literature
历史（lì shǐ）history
法律（fǎ lǜ）law
经济（jīng jì）economy
数学（shù xué）math

化学（huà xué）chemistry
物理（wù lǐ）physics
生物（shēng wù）biology
政治（zhèng zhì）politics
地理（dì lǐ）geography
外语（wài yǔ）foreign language
哲学（zhé xué）philosophy
心理学（xīn lǐ xué）psychology
国家（guó jiā）country
中国（zhōng guó）China
中国人（zhōng guó rén）Chinese
英国（yīng guó）Britain
美国（měi guó）America
加拿大（jiā ná dà）Canada
德国（dé guó）Germany
法国（fǎ guó）France
意大利（yì dà lì）Italy
日本（rì běn）Japan
俄罗斯（é luó sī）Russia
韩国（hán guó）South Korea
澳大利亚（ào dà lì yà）Australia
新西兰（xīn xī lán）New Zealand
丹麦（dān mài）Denmark
荷兰（hé lán）Holland
挪威（nuó wēi）Norway
瑞典（ruì diǎn）Sweden
瑞士（ruì shì）Switzerland
西班牙（xī bān yá）Spain
葡萄牙（pú táo yá）Portugal
希腊（xī là）Greece

土耳其（tǔ ěr qí）Turkey

伊朗（yī lǎng）Iran

伊拉克（yī lā kè）Iraq

巴西（bā xī）Brazil

阿根廷（ā gēn tíng）Argentina

泰国（tài guó）Thailand

菲律宾（fēi lǜ bīn）the Philippines

新加坡（xīn jiā pō）Singapore

马来西亚（mǎ lái xī yà）Malaysia

印度尼西亚（yìn dù ní xī yà）Indonesia

肯尼亚（kěn ní yà）Kenya

埃及（āi jí）Egypt

坦桑尼亚（tǎn sāng ní yà）Tanzania

南非（nán fēi）South Africa

印度（yìn dù）India

巴基斯坦（bā jī sī tǎn）Pakistan

斯里兰卡（sī lǐ lán kǎ）Sri Lanka

时间（shí jiān）time

生日（shēng rì）birthday

年（nián）year

月（yuè）month

星期（xīng qī）week

周（zhōu）week

日（rì）day

天（tiān）day

前天（qián tiān）the day before yesterday

昨天（zuó tiān）yesterday

今天（jīn tiān）today

明天（míng tiān）tomorrow

后天（hòu tiān）the day after tomorrow

周末（zhōu mò）weekend
时候（shí hòu）time
现在（xiàn zài）present, now
早晨（zǎo chén）morning
中午（zhōng wǔ）noon
下午（xià wǔ）afternoon
晚上（wǎn shàng）evening, night
一会儿（yī huìr）a little while
好久（hǎo jiǔ）for a long time
小时（xiǎo shí）hour
分钟（fèn zhōng）minute
秒（miǎo）second
地方（dì fang）place
免税店（miǎn shuì diàn）duty-free shop
学校（xué xiào）school
公园（gōng yuán）park
游乐园（yóu lè yuán）amusement park
动物园（dòng wù yuán）zoo
电影院（diàn yǐng yuàn）cinema, movie theater
图书馆（tú shū guǎn）library
广场（guǎng chǎng）square, plaza
银行（yín háng）bank
医院（yī yuàn）hospital
诊所（zhěn suǒ）clinic
机场（jī chǎng）airport
邮局（yóu jú）post office
火车站（huǒ chē zhàn）train station
汽车站（qì chē zhàn）bus station
码头（mǎ tóu）dock
酒店（jiǔ diàn）hotel

餐馆（cān guǎn）restaurant
咖啡馆（kā fēi guǎn）coffee house
茶楼（chá lóu）tea house
警察局（jǐng chá jú）police office
监狱（jiān yù）jail
商店（shāng diàn）store
市场（shì chǎng）market
超市（chāo shì）supermarket
夜总会（yè zǒng huì）nightclub
酒吧（jiǔ ba）bar
音乐会（yīn yuè huì）concert
大学（dà xué）university
书店（shū diàn）bookstore
花店（huā diàn）florist
百货商店（bǎi huò shāng diàn）department store
首饰店（shǒu shì diàn）jewelry store
服装店（fú zhuāng diàn）boutique
五金店（wǔ jīn diàn）hardware store
纪念品店（jì niàn pǐn diàn）souvenir shop
面包房（miàn bāo fáng）bakery
蛋糕店（dàn gāo diàn）cake shop
停车场（tíng chē chǎng）parking lot
加油站（jiā yóu zhàn）gas station
市政厅（shì zhèng tīng）town hall
博物馆（bó wù guǎn）museum
艺术馆（yì shù guǎn）art gallery
星巴克（xīng bā kè）Starbucks
肯德基（kěn dé jī）KFC
麦当劳（mài dāng láo）McDonalds
汉堡王（hàn bǎo wáng）Burger King

米其林（mǐ qí lín）Michelin
必胜客（bì shèng kè）Pizza Hut
喜来登酒店（xǐ lái dēng jiǔ diàn）Sharaton Hotel
希尔顿酒店（xī ěr dùn jiǔ diàn）Hilton Hotel
香格里拉酒店（xiāng gé lǐ lā jiǔ diàn）Shangri-la Hotel
公司（gōng sī）company
工厂（gōng chǎng）factory
车间（chē jiān）workshop
办公室（bàn gōng shì）office
天安门广场（tiān ān mén guǎng chǎng）Tiananmen Square
故宫（gù gōng）Forbidden City
长城（cháng chéng）Great Wall
钱（qián）money
现金（xiàn jīn）cash
零钱（líng qián）change
发票（fā piào）invoice
汇率（huì lǜ）exchange rate
取款机（qǔ kuǎn jī）cash machine
信用卡（xìn yòng kǎ）credit card
人民币（rén mín bì）Chinese *yuan*
美金（měi jīn）US dollar
港币（gǎng bì）Hong Kong dollar
日元（rì yuán）yen
英镑（yīng bàng）pound
欧元（ōu yuán）euro
护照（hù zhào）passport
飞机（fēi jī）airplane
出租车（chū zū chē）taxi
自行车（zì xíng chē）bike
摩托车（mó tuo chē）motor bike

火车（huǒ chē）train

救护车（jiù hù chē）ambulance

消防车（xiāo fáng chē）fire engine

警车（jǐng chē）police car

卡车（kǎ chē）truck

餐车（cān chē）dining car

列车卧铺（liè chē wò pù）sleeper car

地铁（dì tiě）subway

公交车（gōng jiāo chē）bus

船（chuán）boat

渡轮（dù lún）ferry

游艇（yóu tǐng）yacht

直升机（zhí shēng jī）helicopter, chopper

车顶行李架（chē dǐng háng lǐ jià）roofrack

儿童座椅（ér tóng zuò yǐ）child seat

行李箱（xíng lǐ xiāng）trunk

轮胎（lún tāi）tire

发动机（fā dòng jī）engine

站台（zhàn tái）platform

航站楼（háng zhàn lóu）terminal

柜台（counter）guì tái

交通信号灯（jiāo tōng xìn hào dēng）traffic light

人行道（rén xíng dào）pedestrian crossing

票（piào）ticket

登机牌（dēng jī pái）boarding pass

自动售票机（zì dòng shòu piào jī）automatic ticket machine

救生衣（jiù shēng yī）life jacket

救生圈（jiù shēng quān）life ring

公路（gōng lù）road

高速公路（gāo sù gōng lù）highway

铁轨（tiě guǐ）rail
收费站（shōu fèi zhàn）toll gate
东边（dōng biān）east
西边（xī biān）west
南边（nán biān）south
北边（běi biān）north
上面（shàng mian）above
下面（xià mian）under
左边（zuǒ biān）left
右边（yòu biān）right
旁边（páng biān）next to
对面（duì miàn）opposite
前面（qián mian）ahead, in front
后面（hòu mian）at the back, behind
里面（lǐ mian）inside
外面（wài mian）outside
路口（lù kǒu）crossing
啤酒（pí jiǔ）beer
红酒（hóng jiǔ）wine
水（shuǐ）water
茶（chá）tea
果汁（guǒ zhī）juice
咖啡（kā fēi）coffee
卡布奇诺（kǎ bù qí nuò）cappuccino
拿铁（ná tiě）latte
可乐（kě lè）coke
雪碧（xuě bì）sprite
芬达（fēn dá）fanta
苏打水（sū dǎ shuǐ）soda
威士忌（wēi shì jì）whisky

白兰地（bái lán dì）brandy

鸡尾酒（jī wěi jiǔ）cocktail

朗姆（lǎng mǔ）rum

白酒（bái jiǔ）white wine

热巧克力（rè qiǎo kè lì）hot chocolate

酸奶（suān nǎi）yogurt

牛奶（niú nǎi）milk

豆奶（dòu nǎi）soy milk

汤（tāng）soup

水果（shuǐ guǒ）fruit

苹果（píng guǒ）apple

香蕉（xiāng jiāo）banana

桔子（jú zi）orange

芒果（máng guǒ）mango

葡萄（pú tao）grape

木瓜（mù guā）papaya

西瓜（xī guā）watermelon

梨（lí）pear

柠檬（níng méng）lemon

青柠（qīng níng）lime

梅子（méi zi）plum

樱桃（yīng tao）cherry

番石榴（fān shí liu）guava

草莓（cǎo méi）strawberry

菠萝（bō luó）pineapple

荔枝（lì zhī）lychee

椰子（yē zi）coconut

桃（táo）peach

枣（zǎo）date

石榴（shí liu）pomegranate

火龙果（huǒ lóng guǒ）pitaya
蔬菜（shū cài）vegetable
茄子（qié zi）eggplant
生菜（shēng cài）lettuce
土豆（tǔ dòu）potato
胡萝卜（hú luó bo）carrot
洋葱（yáng cōng）onion
韭菜（jiǔ cài）leek
黄瓜（huáng guā）cucumber
西红柿（xī hóng shì）tomato
芹菜（qín cài）celery
西兰花（xī lán huā）broccoli
玉米（yù mǐ）corn
大白菜（dà bái cài）cabbage
莴笋（wō sǔn）asparagus
青椒（qīng jiāo）green pepper
海带（hǎi dài）seaweed
葱（cōng）green onion
姜（jiāng）ginger
蒜（suàn）garlic
菜单（cài dān）menu
早饭（zǎo fàn）breakfast
午饭（wǔ fàn）lunch
晚饭（wǎn fàn）dinner
零食（líng shí）snack
鸡蛋（jī dàn）egg
肉（ròu）meat
鸡（jī）chicken
鹅（é）goose
鱼（yú）fish

鸭（yā）duck

猫（māo）cat

狗（gǒu）dog

鹿（lù）deer

驴（lǘ）donkey

猴（hóu）monkey

海鲜（hǎi xiān）sea food

牛肉（niú ròu）beef

螃蟹（páng xiè）crab

牛排（niú pái）steak

虾（xiā）shrimp

猪肉（zhū ròu）pork

鱿鱼（yóu yú）squid

羊肉（yáng ròu）mutton

糖（táng）sugar

盐（yán）salt

醋（cù）vinegar

酱油（jiàng yóu）soy sauce

胡椒（hú jiāo）pepper

面包（miàn bāo）bread

果酱（guǒ jiàng）jam

奶油（nǎi yóu）cream

奶酪（nǎi lào）cheese

黄油（huáng yóu）butter

香肠（xiāng cháng）sausage

米饭（mǐ fàn）cooked rice

馄饨（hún tun）wontons

饺子（jiǎo zi）dumplings

包子（bāo zi）steamed dumplings

面条（miàn tiáo）noodles

月饼（yuè bǐng）mooncake
汉堡（hàn bǎo）hamburger
热狗（rè gǒu）hot dog
薯条（shǔ tiáo）French fries
炸鸡（zhá jī）fried chicken
三明治（sān míng zhì）sandwich
橄榄（gǎn lǎn）olive
坚果（jiān guǒ）nut
虾片（xiā piàn）prawn cracker
沙拉（shā lā）salad
爆米花（bào mǐ huā）popcorn
甜点（tián diǎn）dessert
冰淇淋（bīng qí lín）ice cream
棒棒糖（bàng bang táng）lolipop
果冻（guǒ dòng）jelly
蛋糕（dàn gāo）cake
衣服（yī fú）clothes
裤子（kù zi）pants
牛仔裤（niú zǎi kù）jeans
T恤（T xù）t-shirt
衬衫（chèn shān）shirt
毛衣（máo yī）sweater
大衣（dà yī）coat
裙子（qún zi）skirt, dress
西装（xī zhuāng）suit
夹克（jiá kè）jacket
背心（bèi xīn）vest
短裤（duǎn kù）shorts
领带（lǐng dài）tie
帽子（mào zi）hat, cap

鞋子（xié zi）shoes

靴子（xuē zi）boots

皮鞋（pí xié）leather shoes

运动鞋（yùn dòng xié）sneakers

高跟鞋（gāo gēn xié）high heels

凉鞋（liáng xié）sandals

人字拖（rén zì tuō）flip-flops

袜子（wà zǐ）socks

内衣（nèi yī）underwear

内裤（nèi kù）panties

项链（xiàng liàn）necklace

手链（shǒu liàn）bracelet

手表（shǒu biǎo）watch

戒指（jiè zhǐ）ring

耳钉（ěr dìng）earring

泳装（yǒng zhuāng）swimsuit

墨镜（mò jìng）sunglasses

遮阳帽（zhē yáng mào）sun hat

眼（yǎn）eye

耳（ěr）ear

口（kǒu）mouth

嘴（zuǐ）mouth

舌头（shé tou）tongue

喉咙（hóu long）throat

鼻（bí）nose

身体（shēn tǐ）body

头（tóu）head

脸（liǎn）face

头发（tóu fa）hair

脖子（bó zi）neck

手臂（shǒu bì）arm
手（shǒu）hand
指甲（zhǐ jia）nail
手腕（shǒu wàn）wrist
肩（jiān）shoulder
胸（xiōng）chest
腹（fù）belly
腿（tuǐ）leg
膝盖（xī gài）knee
脚（jiǎo）foot
脚踝（jiǎo huái）ankle
中药（zhōng yào）traditional Chinese medicine
西药（xī yào）Western medicine
绷带（bēng dài）bandage
创可贴（chuàng kě tiē）adhesive bandage
胶囊（jiāo náng）capsule
药片（yào piàn）pill
吸入器（xī rù qì）inhaler
栓剂（shuān jì）suppository
滴剂（dī jì）drop
喷雾器（pēn wù qì）spray
糖浆（táng jiāng）syrup
软膏（ruǎn gāo）ointment
足球（zú qiú）football
护腕（hù wàn）wristbands
乒乓球（pīng pāng qiú）ping pong
乒乓球拍（pīng pāng qiú pāi）table tennis bat
网球（wǎng qiú）tennis
网球拍（wǎng qiú pāi）tennis racket
高尔夫球（gāo ěr fū qiú）golf

高尔夫球杆（gāo ěr fū qiú gān）golf club
羽毛球（yǔ máo qiú）badminton
篮球（lán qiú）basketball
排球（pái qiú）volleyball
体操（tǐ cāo）gymnastics
武术（wǔ shù）martial art, kung fu
跆拳道（tái quán dào）taekwondo
房子（fáng zi）house
楼（lóu）building
电梯（diàn tī）elevator
家（jiā）home
门（mén）door
房间（fáng jiān）room
房间号（fáng jiān hào）room number
日用品（rì yòng pǐn）articles for daily use
口红（kǒu hóng）lipstick
香水（xiāng shuǐ）perfume
筷子（kuài zi）chopstick
刀子（dāo zi）knife
叉子（chā zi）fork
勺子（sháo zi）spoon
餐巾（cān jīn）napkin
纸巾（zhǐ jīn）tissue
盘子（pán zi）plate
碗（wǎn）bowl
杯子（bēi zi）cup
酒杯（jiǔ bēi）glass
词典（cí diǎn）dictionary
名片（míng piàn）business card
便签（biàn qiān）note pad

公文包（gōng wén bāo）briefcase
打印机（dǎ yìn jī）printer
传真机（chuán zhēn jī）fax machine
锁（suǒ）lock
伞（sǎn）umbrella
圆珠笔（yuán zhū bǐ）gel pen
颜色（yán sè）color
礼物（lǐ wù）gift
箱子（xiāng zǐ）case
小冰箱（xiǎo bīng xiāng）min bar
衣橱（yī chú）wardrobe
茶几（chá jǐ）tea table
沙发（shā fā）sofa
椅子（yǐ zǐ）chair
餐桌（cān zhuō）dining table
床（chuáng）bed
被子（bèi zi）quilt
枕头（zhěn tóu）pillow
毯子（tǎn zi）blanket
灯泡（dēng pào）light bulb
插头转换器（chā tóu zhuǎn huàn qì）adapter
电水壶（diàn shuǐ hú）kettle
散热器（sàn rè qì）radiator
挂衣架（guà yī jià）hanger
遥控器（yáo kòng qì）remote control
窗帘（chuāng lián）blind
浴缸（yù gāng）bathtub
肥皂（féi zào）soap
毛巾（máo jīn）towel
浴袍（yù páo）robe

沐浴乳（mù yù rǔ）shower gel
牙膏（yá gāo）toothpaste
牙刷（yá shuā）toothbrash
润肤露（rùn fū lù）body lotion
漱口水（shù kǒu shuǐ）mouthwash
剃须刀（tì xū dāo）razor
剃须泡沫（tì xū pào mù）shaving foam
吹风机（chuī fēng jī）hairdryer
洗发水（xǐ fà shuǐ）shampoo
护发素（hù fà sù）conditioner
指甲刀（zhǐ jiǎ dāo）nail clipper
指甲剪（zhǐ jiǎ jiǎn）nail scissor
梳子（shū zi）comb
风扇（fēng shàn）fan
空调（kōng tiáo）air-conditioner
微波炉（wēi bō lú）microwave
熨斗（yùn dòu）iron
熨衣板（yùn yī bǎn）ironing board
拖把（tuō bǎ）mop
水桶（shuǐ tǒng）bucket
洗衣机（xǐ yī jī）washing machine
冰箱（bīng xiāng）refrigerator
垃圾桶（lā jī tǒng）garbage can
锁（suǒ）lock
钥匙（yào shi）key
烟雾报警器（yān wù bào jǐng qì）smoke alarm
灭火器（miè huǒ qì）fire extinguisher
开瓶器（kāi píng qì）bottle opener
案板（àn bǎn）cutting board
菜刀（cài dāo）kitchen knife

削皮刀（xiāo pí dāo）peeler
打蛋器（dǎ dàn qì）whisk
煎锅（jiān guō）frying pan
砂锅（shā guō）casserole dish
搅拌器（jiǎo bàn qì）blender
烤盘（kǎo pán）cookie sheet
烤箱手套（kǎo xiāng shǒu tào）oven mitts
围裙（wéi qún）apron
推车（tuī chē）grocery cart
篮子（lán zi）basket
打火机（dǎ huǒ jī）lighter
香烟（xiāng yān）cigarette
雪茄（xuě jiā）cigar
烟灰缸（yān huī gāng）ashtray
相机（xiàng jī）camera
相册（xiàng cè）photo album
键盘（jiàn pán）keyboard
鼠标（shǔ biāo）mouse
路由器（lù yóu qì）router
无线网络（wú xiàn wǎng luò）WIFI
密码（mì mǎ）password
书（shū）book
纸（zhǐ）paper
笔（bǐ）pen
铅笔（qiān bǐ）pencil
本子（běn zi）notebook
东西（dōng xi）thing
跨包（kuà bāo）purse
背包（bèi bāo）bag
钱包（qián bāo）wallet

天然气（tiān rán qì）natural gas

电（diàn）electricity

电话（diàn huà）telephone

号码（hào mǎ）number

手机（shǒu jī）mobile

电视（diàn shì）television

电脑（diàn nǎo）computer

笔记本电脑（bǐ jì běn diàn nǎo）lap top

口香糖（kǒu xiāng táng）gum

杂志（zá zhì）magazine

报纸（bào zhǐ）newspaper

小说（xiǎo shuō）novel

漫画（màn huà）comic book

电影（diàn yǐng）movie

Glossary of Verbs

是（shì）to be

有（yǒu）to have

做（zuò）to do

会（huì）can, could, will, would, shall, should

说（shuō）to speak, to say

要（yào）to take, to want, will, would

去（qù）to go

看（kàn）to see, to look at

知道（zhī dào）to know

带（dài）to take, to bring

想（xiǎng）to want, to miss

来（lái）to come

给（gěi）to give

成（chéng）to become, to be done

用（yòng）to use

找（zhǎo）to find
告诉（gào sù）to tell
求（qiú）to beg
埋（mái）to bury
讲（jiǎng）to tell, to speak
离开（lí kāi）to leave
需要（xū yào）to require, to need
工作（gōng zuò）to work
感觉（gǎn jué）to feel
问（wèn）to ask
展示（zhǎn shì）to show
试（shì）to try
叫（jiào）to shout, to call
提供（tí gòng）to offer, to provide
保持（bǎo chí）to keep
拿（ná）to take
转（zhuǎn）to turn
跟（gēn）to follow
喜欢（xǐ huān）to like
帮（bāng）to help
跑（pǎo）to run
走（zǒu）to walk
写（xiě）to write
动（dòng）to move
玩（wán）to play
付（fù）to pay
听（tīng）to listen
相信（xiàng xìn）to believe
允许（yǔn xǔ）to allow
遇见（yù jiàn）to meet

住（zhù）to live

站（zhàn）to stand

发生（fā shēng）to happen, to take place

拉（lā）to pull

推（tuī）to push

说话（shuō huà）to speak

出现（chū xiàn）to appear

生产（shēng chǎn）to produce

考虑（kǎo lǜ）to consider

建议（jiàn yì）to suggest

期望（qī wàng）to expect

让（ràng）to let

喊（hǎn）to shout

丢（diū）to lose

加（jiā）to add

改变（gǎi biàn）to change

记（jì）to note, to write

买（mǎi）to buy, to purchase

卖（mài）to sell

录（lù）to record

送（sòng）to deliver, to give (as a present)

收（shōu）to collect

决定（jué dìng）to decide

赢（yíng）to win

明白（míng bái）to understand

发展（fā zhǎn）to develop

描述（miáo shù）to describe

同意（tóng yì）to agree

开（kāi）to open, to drive

关（guān）to close

到（dào）to arrive, to reach
建（jiàn）to build
还（huán）to return
画（huà）to draw
希望（xī wàng）to wish, to hope
创造（chuàng zào）to create
等（děng）to wait
造成（zào chéng）to cause
通过（tōng guò）to pass
撒谎（sā huǎng）to lie
接受（jiē shòu）to accept
举（jǔ）to raise, to lift
申请（shēn qǐng）to apply
打（dǎ）to hit, to punch
学习（xué xí）to learn
解释（jiě shì）to explain
借（jiè）to borrow
成长（chéng zhǎng）to grow
上报（shàng bào）to report
宣布（xuān bù）to announce
支持（zhī chí）to support
切（qiē）to cut
形成（xíng chéng）to form
呆（dāi）to stay
减少（jiǎn shǎo）to reduce, to decrease
建立（jiàn lì）to establish
加入（jiā rù）to join
寻求（xún qiú）to seek
实现（shí xiàn）to realize
选择（xuǎn zé）to choose

面对（miàn duì）to face

供应（gōng yīng）to supply

终结（zhōng jié）to end

生（shēng）to give birth

驾驶（jià shǐ）to drive

代表（dài biǎo）to represent

讨论（tǎo lùn）to discuss

放置（fàng zhì）to place

爱（ài）to love

捡（jiǎn）to pick spmething up from the ground

证明（zhèng míng）to prove

穿（chuān）to wear

争吵（zhēng chǎo）to argue

抓（zhuā）to seize, to grasp

欣赏（xīn shǎng）to enjoy

介绍（jiè shào）to introduce

吃（chī）to eat

进（jìn）to enter

退（tuì）to retreat, to move back

出席（chū xí）to attend

指（zhǐ）to point

计划（jì huá）to plan

演（yǎn）to act

影响（yǐng xiǎng）to influence

管理（guǎn lǐ）to manage

识别（shí bié）to identify

谢（xiè）to thank

比较（bǐ jiào）to compare

忘（wàng）to forget

暗示（àn shì）to indicate

加强（jiā qiáng）to strengthen
遭受（zāo shòu）to suffer
出版（chū bǎn）to publish
表达（biǎo dá）to express
躲避（duǒ bì）to avoid, to dodge
完成（wán chéng）to complete, to finish
节省（jiē shěng）to save
设计（shè jì）to design
对待（duì dài）to treat
分享（fèn xiǎng）to share
控制（kòng zhì）to control
移除（yí chú）to remove
拜访（bài fǎng）to visit
扔（rēng）to throw
存在（cún zài）to exist
鼓励（gǔ lì）to encourage
强迫（qiáng pò）to force
反映（fǎn yìng）to reflect
笑（xiào）to smile
哭（kū）to cry
承认（chéng rèn）to admit
假设（jiǎ shè）to assume
代替（dài tì）to replace
准备（zhǔn bèi）to prepare
提高（tí gāo）to improve
填（tián）to fill
提及（tí jí）to mention
打架（dǎ jià）to fight
拒绝（jù jué）to refuse
阻止（zǔ zhǐ）to prevent

教（jiāo）to teach
躺（tǎng）to lie down
揭示（jiē shì）to reveal
陈述（chén shù）to state
操作（cāo zuò）to operate
回答（huí dá）to answer
记录（jì lù）to record
检查（jiǎn chá）to check
释放（shì fàng）to release
延长（yán cháng）to extend
修（xiū）to fix
飞（fēi）to fly
摇（yáo）to shake
签（qiān）to sign
保护（bǎo hù）to protect
适应（shì yìng）to get used to
确认（què rèn）to confirm
协调（xié tiáo）to coordinate
嫁（jià）to marry (female to male)
娶（qǔ）to marry (male to female)
照顾（zhào gù）to take care of
收集（shōu jí）to collect
雇（gù）to hire, to employ
标（biāo）to mark
否认（fǒu rèn）to deny
射（shè）to shoot
瞄准（miáo zhǔn）to aim at
任命（rèn mìng）to appoint
订（dìng）to order
观察（guān chá）to observe

喝（hē）to drink
忽略（hū luè）to ignore
安排（ān pái）to arrange
关注（guān zhù）to focus
尝（cháng）to taste

Part 2: Mastering Chinese Words

Expanding Your Vocabulary with 2500 of the Most Common Chinese Words

Introduction

Within China, there are 56 nationalities, so you might be wondering what exactly is "Chinese language"? Well, it is "Han language".

In China, the Han population is the largest. The other 55 nationalities are referred to as minorities. As most people use the Han language, it has become the main tool for communication between the different nationalities.

The Chinese language has its own pronunciation and characters. Even though the Chinese people use the same characters, they may differ in their pronunciation from place to place because of the sheer size of the country. As a result, many dialects exist within China, e.g., Shanghai dialect, Guangdong dialect (Cantonese), etc. If a person from Shanghai uses the Shanghai dialect in Guangdong, few people would understand what is being said. This would also apply to people speaking Cantonese in Shanghai. Different dialects can make communication very difficult.

After the foundation of the People's Republic of China in 1949, the government made great efforts to spread Putonghua (Mandarin), the common language. Putonghua is now called "Modern Chinese". Pronunciation of Putonghua is based on the Beijing dialect, and the vocabulary is based on the north Chinese language. Now, Chinese people mainly use Putonghua to communicate. The Chinese language that you will learn in this book is Putonghua.

Learning Chinese characters is difficult, and because of this, people often lack the motivation to continue learning. In fact, to learn Chinese, it is not essential to learn the characters. To communicate verbally is often the learner's desire. Based on this, this book was created to expand your vocabulary. Usually, Chinese textbooks rely on learners to learn the characters. But here, Pinyin is introduced, allowing learners quickly to remember every word.

Now it is time to commence your lessons and learn the fascinating language of the Chinese.

Good luck!

Section 1

1,200 BASIC WORDS

A word is the smallest meaningful unit in a language. Words are used as basic building blocks to express ideas. In this chapter, you will learn 1,200 basic words.

Chinese words represented by a single syllable are called monosyllabic words. Words represented by two syllables are called dissyllabic words. Words composed of three or more syllables are called polysyllabic words. In writing, a syllable is a character. As such, monosyllabic words are represented by one character, dissyllabic words by two, and polysyllabic words by more than two.

Chinese words can be divided into two kinds: notional and function words. Nouns, verbs, auxiliary verbs, adjectives, numerals, measure words, and pronouns belong to the notional word category. Adverbs, prepositions, conjunctions, particles, interjections, and onomatopes belong to the function word category.

Normally, a word belongs to a certain part of speech. Some words, however, have the grammatical function of two or more parts of speech. Remember to pay more attention to these words.

You shall deal with each part of speech separately.

Chapter 1. Nouns

In Chinese, the same form of a noun is used in the subject and object position. Except for the written form of third-person pronouns, Chinese nouns are not gendered, and there is no distinction between masculine, feminine, and neuter found in many European languages.

1. 家/jiā/ – home
2. 学校/xué xiào/ – school
3. 饭馆/fàn guǎn/ – restaurant
4. 餐厅/cān tīng/ – dining room; dining hall; restaurant
5. 商店/shāng diàn/ – shop; store
6. 医院/yī yuàn/ – hospital
7. 火车站/huǒ chē zhàn/ – train station
8. 公司/gōng sī/ – company
9. 机场/jī chǎng/ – airport
10. 教室/jiāo shì/ – classroom
11. 房间/fáng jiān/ – room
12. 路/lù/ – road; path
13. 超市/chāo shì/ – supermarket
14. 入口/rù kǒu/ – entrance
15. 公园/gōng yuán/ – park

16. 花园/huā yuán/ - garden
17. 图书馆/tú shū guǎn/ - library
18. 办公室/bàn gōng shì/ - office
19. 厨房/chú fáng/ - kitchen
20. 洗手间/xǐ shǒu jiān/ - washroom; toilet; lavatory
21. 厕所/cè suǒ/ - toilet
22. 银行/yín háng/ - bank
23. 宾馆/bīn guǎn/ - hotel
24. 加油站/jiā yóu zhàn/ - gas station
25. 大使馆/dà shǐ guǎn/ - embassy
26. 市场/shì chǎng/ - market
27. 长城/cháng chéng/ - the Great Wall
28. 长江/cháng jiāng/ - the Yangtze River
29. 黄河/huáng hé/ - Yellow River
30. 地方/dì fāng/ - place; region
31. 街道/jiē dào/ - street
32. 农村/nóng cūn/ - countryside; village
33. 城市/chéng shì/ - city
34. 北京/běi jīng/ - Beijing
35. 首都/shǒu dōu/ - capital
36. 省/shěng/ - province; to save

我们得想一种省钱的办法。- We have to think of a way to save money.

37. 中国/zhōng guó/ - China
38. 国家/guó jiā/ - country
39. 亚洲/yà zhōu/ - Asia
40. 世界/shì jiè/ - world
41. 地球/dì qiú/ - the Earth
42. 地点/dì diǎn/ - place; location
43. 上/shàng/ - up; on; last (week, etc.); Part I (of two parts)

书在桌子上。- The book is on the table.

我上周去了医院。- I went to the hospital last week.

《哈利·波特与死亡圣器·上》- Harry Potter and the Deathly Hallows Part I

44. 下/xià/ - down; under; below; next (week, month, year); Part II (of two parts)

他们在地下发现财宝。- They found treasure under the ground.

我下周要去北京。- I'm going to Beijing next week.

《哈利·波特与死亡圣器·下》- Harry Potter and the Deathly Hallows Part II

45. 前面/qián miàn/ - ahead; in front; preceding

46. 后面/hòu miàn/ - back; behind; afterward

47. 里/lǐ/ - inside; interior; Chinese mile (measure unit, 500 meters)

48. 左边/zuǒ biān/ - left side

49. 右边/yòu biān/ - right side

50. 外/wài/ - outside; external; foreign

51. 旁边/páng biān/ - side; to the side; beside

52. 中间/zhōng jiān/ - middle; between

我想要中间那个。- I want the middle one.

我不希望我们中间有秘密。- I don't want any secrets between us.

53. 附近/fù jìn/ - nearby; (in the) vicinity

54. 东/dōng/ - east

55. 西/xī/ - west

56. 南/nán/ - south

57. 北方/běi fāng/ - north; the northern part of a country

58. 周围/zhōu wéi/ - surroundings

59. 对面/duì miàn/ - opposite

60. 内/nèi/ - inside; internal

61. 底/dǐ/ - bottom; the end of (a period of time)

把洋葱片铺在盘底。 - Spread the onion slices on the bottom of the dish.

我月底还你钱。 - I'll pay you back at the end of this month.

62. 今天/jīn tiān/ - today

63. 明天/míng tiān/ - tomorrow

64. 昨天/zuó tiān/ - yesterday

65. 上午/shàng wǔ/ - morning

66. 中午/zhōng wǔ/ - noon; midday

67. 下午/xià wǔ/ - afternoon

68. 年/nián/ - year

69. 月/yuè/ - month; moon

70. 日/rì/ - day; sun

71. 星期/xīng qī/ - week

72. 点/diǎn/ - o'clock; dot; to order; to light (cigarette, fire, etc.)

八点了。 - It is eight o'clock.

用绿点对它们进行了标记。 - Mark them with a green dot.

她点了一份沙拉。 - She ordered a salad.

如果我们抽烟的话，最好点一支让她也试试。 - If we're going to smoke, we'd better light one and let her try it out as well.

73. 分钟/fēn zhōng/ - minute

74. 现在/xiàn zài/ - now; at present; at the moment

75. 时候/shí hòu/ - time; moment; period

你什么时候来？ - What time will you be here?

76. 早上/zǎo shàng/ - morning

77. 晚上/wǎn shàng/ - evening; night

78. 小时/xiǎo shí/ - hour

79. 时间/shí jiān/ - time

80. 去年/qù nián/ - last year

81. 号/hào/ - day of month; (suffix used after) name of a ship; number

今天是二月二十号。- Today is February 20.

我最喜欢的电影是泰坦尼克号。- My favorite movie is *Titanic*.

你的房间号是 606. - Your room number is 606.

82. 生日/shēng rì/ - birthday

83. 春/chūn/ - spring

84. 夏/xià/ - summer

85. 秋/qiū/ - autumn

86. 冬/dōng/ - winter

87. 季节/jì jié/ - season

88. 以前/yǐ qián/ - ago; previous; before; previous

89. 以后/yǐ hòu/ - later on

90. 过去/guò qù/ - (in the) past; previous; to pass by; to go over

91. 最近/zuì jìn/ - recently; lately; these days; nearest (of locations): shortest (of routes)

92. 周末/zhōu mò/ - weekend

93. 刚才/gāng cái/ - just now; a while ago

94. 将来/jiāng lái/ - future; in the future

95. 后来/hòu lái/ - afterward; later

96. 平时/píng shí/ - in normal times

97. 当时/dāng shí/ - at that time

98. 寒假/hán jiǎ/ - winter vacation

101. 人/rén/ - person; people; human

102. 男人/nán rén/ - man

103. 女人/nǚ rén/ - woman

104. 先生/xiān shēng/ - sir; Mr.

105. 小姐/xiǎo jiě/ - Miss; prostitute (slang)

106. 儿童/ér tóng/ - children

107. 爸爸/bà ba/ - dad; father

108. 父亲/fù qīn/ - father (written)
109. 妈妈/mā ma/ - mom; mother
110. 母亲/mǔ qīn/ - mother (written)
111. 儿子/ér zi/ - son
112. 女儿/nǚ ér/ - daughter
113. 爷爷/yé ye/ - grandfather (paternal)
114. 奶奶/nǎi nai/ - grandmother (paternal)
115. 孙子/sūn zi/ - grandson
116. 叔叔/shū shu/ - uncle; paternal younger brother
117. 阿姨/ā yí/ - aunt
118. 哥哥/gē ge/ - older brother
119. 姐姐/jiě jie/ - older sister
120. 弟弟/dì di/ - younger brother
121. 妹妹/mèi mei/ - younger sister
122. 丈夫/zhàng fu/ - husband
123. 妻子/qī zǐ/ - wife
124. 孩子/hái zi/ - child; kid
125. 亲戚/qīn qi/ - relative; kinsfolk
126. 老师/lǎo shī/ - teacher
127. 学生/xué shēng/ - student
128. 同学/tóng xué/ - classmate
129. 朋友/péng yǒu/ - friend
130. 医生/yī shēng/ - doctor
131. 服务员/fú wù yuán/ - waiter; waitress
132. 同事/tóng shì/ - colleague; coworker
133. 校长/xiào zhǎng/ - headmaster
134. 经理/jīng lǐ/ - manager
135. 司机/sī jī/ - driver
136. 邻居/lín jū/ - neighbor
137. 房东/fáng dǒng/ - landlord

138. 客人/kè rén/ - guest; customer
139. 师傅/shī fu/ - master
140. 演员/yǎn yuán/ - actor; actress
141. 警察/jǐng chá/ - police officer
142. 记者/jì zhě/ - journalist
143. 大夫/dài fu/ - doctor
144. 护士/hù shì/ - nurse
145. 顾客/gù kè/ - client; customer
146. 观众/guān zhòng/ - audience
147. 作者/zuò zhě/ - writer
148. 作家/zuò jiā/ - author
149. 教授/jiāo shòu/ - professor

委员会由教授和工程师组成。- The committee was composed of professors and engineers.

/jiāo shòu/ - to instruct; to teach

他们将教授阅读、写作和语法基础知识。- They will teach the basics of reading, writing, and grammar.

150. 研究生/yán jiū shēng/ - graduate student
151. 硕士/shuò shì/ - master's degree
152. 博士/bó shì/ - doctor; Ph.D.
153. 律师/lǜ shī/ - lawyer
154. 导游/dǎo yóu/ - tour guide
155. 售货员/shòu huò yuán/ - salesclerk; shop assistant
156. 衣服/yī fu/ - clothes
157. 衬衫/chèn shān/ - shirt
158. 裤子/kù zi/ - pants
159. 裙子/qún zi/ - skirt
160. 帽子/mào zi/ - hat; cap
161. 鞋/xié/ - shoes
162. 皮鞋/pí xié/ - leather shoes

163. 袜子/wà zi/ - socks
164. 眼镜/yǎn jìng/ - glasses
165. 饮料/yǐn liào/ - beverage; drink
166. 水/shuǐ/ - water
167. 茶/chá/ - tea
168. 啤酒/pí jiǔ/ - beer
169. 果汁/guǒ zhī/ - juice
170. 咖啡/kā fēi/ - coffee
171. 汤/tāng/ - soup
172. 食品/shí pǐn/ - food
173. 水果/shuǐ guǒ/ - fruit
174. 苹果/píng guǒ/ - apple
175. 西红柿/xī hóng shì/ - tomato
176. 香蕉/xiāng jiāo/ - banana
177. 葡萄/pú táo/ - grape
178. 西瓜/xī guā/ - watermelon
179. 菜/cài/ - vegetable; dish (type of food)
我不喜欢吃菜。- I don't like eating vegetables.
今晚上有几道菜？- How many dishes will be served tonight?
180. 米饭/mǐ fàn/ - (cooked) rice
181. 米/mǐ/ - rice; meter
182. 面条/miàn tiáo/ - noodles
183. 面包/miàn bāo/ - bread
184. 包子/bāo zi/ - steamed stuffed bun
185. 蛋糕/dàn gāo/ - cake
186. 糖/táng/ - sugar; sweet
187. 羊肉/yáng ròu/ - mutton
188. 牛奶/niú nǎi/ - milk
189. 鸡蛋/jī dàn/ - chicken egg
190. 饺子/jiǎo zi/ - dumpling

191. 盐/yán/ - salt
192. 巧克力/qiǎo kè lì/ - chocolate
193. 饼干/bǐng gàn/ - biscuit; cracker
194. 药/yào/ - pill; medicine
195. 植物/zhí wù/ - plant
196. 叶子/yè zi/ - leaf
197. 身体/shēn tǐ/ - body
198. 眼睛/yǎn jīng/ - eye
199. 头发/tóu fā/ - hair (on the head)
200. 脸/liǎn/ - face
201. 耳朵/ěr duo/ - ear
202. 口/kǒu/ - mouth; measure word for wells, woks, etc.
203. 嘴/zuǐ/ - mouth; beak; spout (of teapot, etc.)
204. 腿/tuǐ/ - leg
205. 胳膊/gē bo/ - arm
206. 脚/jiǎo/ - foot
207. 肚子/dù zi/ - belly
208. 鼻子/bí zi/ - nose
209. 皮肤/pí fū/ - skin
210. 血/xuè; xiě/ - blood
211. 汗/hàn/ - sweat
212. 动物/dòng wù/ - animal
213. 熊猫/xióng māo/ - panda
214. 鸟/niǎo/ - bird
215. 马/mǎ/ - horse
216. 老虎/lǎo hǔ/ - tiger
217. 猴子/hóu zi/ - monkey
218. 猪/zhū/ - pig
219. 狮子/shī zi/ - lion
220. 鱼/yú/ - fish

221. 猫/māo/ - cat

222. 狗/gǒu/ - dog

223. 河/hé/ - river

224. 树/shù/ - tree

225. 草/cǎo/ - grass; draft (of a document)

在写报告前我喜欢先打草。- Before writing a report, I like to make a draft.

226. 云/yún/ - cloud

227. 天气/tiān qì/ - weather

228. 雪/xuě/ - snow

229. 太阳/tài yáng/ - sun

230. 月亮/yuè liàng/ - moon

231. 空气/kōng qì/ - air

232. 阳光/yáng guāng/ - sunshine; sunlight

233. 海洋/hǎi yáng/ - sea; ocean

234. 火/huǒ/ - fire; to be popular; to be furious

这屋里有火。- There is fire in this room.

这部电影非常火。- This movie is very popular.

听到有人背后说他坏话，他火了。- After hearing someone speak ill of him behind his back, he became furious.

235. 森林/sēn lín/ - forest

236. 桥/qiáo/ - bridge

237. 公共汽车/gōng gòng qì chē/ - bus

238. 船/chuán/ - boat; ship; vessel

239. 飞机/fēi jī/ - plane

240. 航班/háng bān/ - flight

241. 出租车/chū zū chē/ - taxi; cab

242. 自行车/zì xíng chē/ - bike; bicycle

243. 地铁/dì tiě/ - subway; underground train

244. 座位/zuò wèi/ - seat

245. 电梯/diàn tī/ – elevator; lift; escalator

246. 楼/lóu/ – building; floor

这是一座写字楼。– This is an office building.

他住在三楼。– He lives on the third floor.

247. 地址/dì zhǐ/ – address

248. 墙/qiáng/ – wall

249. 窗户/chuāng hù/ – window

250. 门/mén/ – door; measure word (for courses, subjects, etc.); Phylum (biology)

开门！– Open the door!

我们这学期有两门新课。– We have two new courses in this semester.

251. 东西/dōng xi/ – thing; direction; person (when talking about someone angrily)

这是什么东西？– What is this thing?

她一出门就东西不分。– As soon as she goes out, she can't tell the direction.

他真不是东西！– He's not a person! (He's a nut!)

252. 家具/jiā jù/ – furniture

253. 桌子/zhuō zi/ – table; desk

254. 椅子/yǐ zi/ – chair

255. 杯子/bēi zi/ – cup; mug

256. 电视/diàn shì/ – television

257. 电脑/diàn nǎo/ – computer

258. 手机/shǒu jī/ – mobile phone

259. 手表/shǒu biǎo/ – watch

260. 报纸/bào zhǐ/ – newspaper

261. 冰箱/bīng xiāng/ – fridge; refrigerator

262. 灯/dēng/ – light; lamp; lantern

263. 伞/sǎn/ – umbrella

264. 盘子/pán zi/ - plate; tray

265. 碗/wǎn/ - bowl

266. 筷子/kuài zi/ - chopsticks

267. 铅笔/qiān bǐ/ - pencil

268. 地图/dì tú/ - map

269. 礼物/lǐ wù/ - gift; present

270. 包/bāo/ - bag; kit; to wrap; to take charge of; to cover; Bao (surname); measure word (for things packed in a bag)

翻包侵犯隐私。- A bag search is an invasion of privacy.

你能帮我把它包起来吗？- Could you help me wrap this?

这件事包在我身上。- I'll take care of this. (Consider it done.)

费用公司包了。- The company will cover the costs.

一包零食 - A bag of snacks

急救包 - First-aid kit

271. 行李箱/xíng lǐ xiāng/ - suitcase

272. 信/xìn/ - letter

273. 书/shū/ - book

274. 照片/zhào piàn/ - photo

275. 照相机/zhào xiàng jī/ - camera

276. 空调/kōng tiáo/ - air conditioner

277. 菜单/cài dān/ - menu

278. 洗衣机/xǐ yī jī/ - washing machine

279. 沙发/shā fā/ - sofa; couch

280. 毛巾/máo jīn/ - towel

281. 牙膏/yá gāo/ - toothpaste

282. 工具/gōng jù/ - tool

283. 刀/dāo/ - knife

284. 镜子/jìng zi/ - mirror

285. 瓶子/píng zi/ - bottle

286. 盒子/hé zi/ - box

287. 塑料袋/sù liào dài/ - plastic bag
288. 钥匙/yào shi/ - key
289. 垃圾桶/lā jī tǒng/ - trash can; dustbin
290. 乒乓球/pīng pāng qiú/ - table tennis; ping pong
291. 羽毛球/yǔ máo qiú/ - badminton
292. 网球/wǎng qiú/ - tennis
293. 信用卡/xìn yòng kǎ/ - credit card
294. 钱/qián/ - money
295. 人民币/rén mín bì/ - RMB; Chinese yuan
296. 票/piào/ - ticket
297. 登机牌/dēng jī pái/ - boarding pass
298. 黑板/hēi bǎn/ - blackboard
299. 电子邮件/diàn zǐ yóu jiàn/ - email
300. 护照/hù zhào/ - passport
301. 签证/qiān zhèng/ - visa
302. 表格/biǎo gé/ - chart; spreadsheet; form
303. 杂志/zá zhì/ - magazine
304. 字典/zì diǎn/ - dictionary
305. 词典/cí diǎn/ - dictionary
306. 笔记本/bǐ jì běn/ - notebook
307. 日记/rì jì/ - diary; journal
308. 文章/wén zhāng/ - article; essay
309. 短信/duǎn xìn/ - text message
310. 报道/bào dào/ - report
311. 名字/míng zì/ - name
312. 汉语/hàn yǔ/ - Chinese (language)
313. 字/zì/ - word; character
314. 题/tí/ - exam question; to inscribe
315. 课/kè/ - class; course
316. 姓/xìng/ - surname

317. 问题/wèn tí/ – question
318. 错误/cuò wù/ – mistake; error
319. 事情/shì qing/ – matter
320. 考试/kǎo shì/ – exam; quiz
321. 意思/yì si/ – meaning
322. 颜色/yán sè/ – color
323. 味道/wèi dào/ – flavor; smell
324. 环境/huán jìng/ – environment; circumstance
325. 句子/jù zi/ – sentence
326. 词语/cí yǔ/ – vocabulary
327. 年级/nián jí/ – grade (at school)
328. 班/bān/ – work shift; class; surname Ban
329. 练习/liàn xí/ – practice; to practice
330. 作业/zuò yè/ – homework; to work

老师布置了很多作业。 – The teacher assigned a lot of homework.

工地上有很多挖掘机正在作业。 – There are many excavators working on the construction site.

331. 历史/lì shǐ/ – history
332. 数学/shù xué/ – math
333. 体育/tǐ yù/ – physical education
334. 音乐/yīn yuè/ – music
335. 爱好/ài hào/ – hobby
336. 比赛/bǐ sài/ – match; race; contest; competition
337. 节目/jiē mù/ – show

我喜欢没有主持人的综艺节目。 – I prefer variety shows without hosts.

338. 演出/yǎn chū/ – to act (in a play); to put on (a performance); to perform.

339. 节 /jié/ - festival; measure word for segments (lessons, wagons, batteries, etc.)

340. 机会 /jī huì/ - opportunity; chance

341. 文化 /wén huà/ - culture

342. 习惯 /xí guàn/ - habit; to get used to

他有很多不好的习惯。 - He has many bad habits.

她习惯天天早起。 - She is used to getting up early.

343. 新闻 /xīn wén/ - news

344. 电影 /diàn yǐng/ - movie

345. 小说 /xiǎo shuō/ - novel

346. 京剧 /jīng jù/ - Beijing Opera

347. 故事 /gù shì/ - story

348. 游戏 /yóu xì/ - game

349. 兴趣 /xìng qù/ - interest

350. 功夫 /gōng fu/ - Kung Fu; time; effort

来一趟费不了你多少功夫。 - It won't take you much time to get here.

做这件事毫不费功夫。 - It doesn't take much effort to do it.

351. 声音 /shēng yīn/ - sound; voice

352. 水平 /shuǐ píng/ - level (of achievement, etc.); horizontal

353. 关系 /guān xi/ - relationship; relation

354. 办法 /bàn fǎ/ - means; method

355. 作用 /zuò yòng/ - function; effect; to act on

这种药有什么作用？ - What effects does this medicine have?

摩擦力作用于运动着的物体，并使其停止。 - Friction acts on moving objects and brings them to a stop.

356. 成绩 /chéng jì/ - achievement; performance records; grades

357. 普通话 /pǔ tōng huà/ - Mandarin

358. 会议 /huì yì/ - meeting; conference

359. 性别 /xìng bié/ - gender; sex

360. 年龄/nián líng/ - (a person's) age

361. 号码/hào mǎ/ - number

你的房间号码是多少？- What's your room number?

362. 数字/shù zì/ - number; figure; digit

363. 气候/qì hòu/ - climate

364. 答案/dá àn/ - answer

365. 广告/guǎng gào/ - advertisement

366. 传真/chuán zhēn/ - fax

367. 自然/zì rán/ - nature; natural; naturally

368. 风景/fēng jǐng/ - scenery

369. 材料/cái liào/ - material

370. 价格/jià gé/ - price

371. 奖金/jiǎng jīn/ - bonus

372. 工资/gōng zī/ - wage; salary

373. 堵车/dǔ chē/ - traffic jam

374. 收入/shōu rù/ - income

375. 部分/bù fen/ - part; section

中国是世界的一部分。- China is a part of the world.

本堂课的第一部分是听力练习。- The first section of this class is to practice your listening skills.

376. 距离/jù lí/ - distance

377. 数量/shù liàng/ - quantity; amount

378. 速度/sù dù/ - speed

379. 方向/fāng xiàng/ - direction

380. 质量/zhì liàng/ - quality

381. 温度/wēn dù/ - temperature

382. 过程/guò chéng/ - process

383. 顺序/shùn xù/ - order

384. 特点/tè diǎn/ - feature; characteristic

385. 效果/xiào guǒ/ - effect

386. 结果/jié guǒ/ - result

387. 目的/mù de/ - target; goal; purpose

388. 关键/guān jiàn/ - key; crucial

这是解决问题的关键。- This is the key to solving the problem.

目前危机正进入决定性的关键阶段。- The crisis is now entering a crucial critical phase.

389. 压力/yā lì/ - pressure

390. 心情/xīn qíng/ - mood

391. 脾气/pí qì/ - temper

392. 动作/dòng zuò/ - action; movement

393. 个子/gè zi/ - (in reference to) one's height or size

他是个大个子。- He's a big guy. (He's a tall guy.)

他个子高。- He's a tall guy.

他是个小个子。- He's a small guy. (He's a short guy.)

他个子矮。- He's a short guy.

394. 好处/hǎo chù/ - benefit

这么做有什么好处？- What are the benefits of doing so?

395. 优点/yōu diǎn/ - advantage

396. 缺点/quē diǎn/ - disadvantage

397. 基础/jī chǔ/ - base; foundation; basis

398. 重点/zhòng diǎn/ - focal point

399. 方法/fāng fǎ/ - method; way

400. 精神/jīng shén/ - spirit; mind (of a person)

401. 感情/gǎn qíng/ - emotion; feeling; relationship

感情不能代替政策。- Emotion should never be a substitute for sound policy.

别伤他的感情。- Don't hurt his feelings.

我们感情很好。- We have a good relationship.

402. 感觉/gǎn jué/ - feeling; to feel; to think

这给了我一种满足的感觉。- It gave me a feeling of satisfaction.

这一幕让你有什么感觉？- How does this make you feel?

我感觉应该这么做。- I think we need to do like this.

403. 印象/yìn xiàng/ - impression

404. 职业/zhí yè/ - occupation; professional

405. 专业/zhuān yè/ - major (at university); specialization; profession

406. 信心/xìn xīn/ - confidence; faith

407. 主意/zhǔ yì/ - idea; plan

408. 理想/lǐ xiǎng/ - ideal; perfection; perfect

409. 样子/yàng zi/ - looks

410. 力气/lì qì/ - strength

411. 态度/tài dù/ - attitude

412. 礼貌/lǐ mào/ - courtesy

413. 能力/néng lì/ - capability; ability

414. 经验/jīng yàn/ - experience

415. 任务/rèn wù/ - mission; assignment; task

416. 技术/jì shù/ - technology; skill

417. 责任/zé rèn/ - responsibility; duty

418. 性格/xìng gé/ - personality; character

419. 条件/tiáo jiàn/ - condition

420. 看法/kàn fǎ/ - viewpoint; opinion; way of looking at a thing

421. 困难/kùn nán/ - difficulty; difficult

422. 交通/jiāo tōng/ - transportation

423. 经济/jīng jì/ - economy; economic

424. 社会/shè huì/ - society

425. 国际/guó jì/ - international

426. 国籍/guó jí/ - nationality

427. 法律/fǎ lǜ/ - law

428. 艺术/yì shù/ - art

429. 科学/kē xué/ - science; scientific

430. 知识/zhī shi/ - knowledge

431. 内容/nèi róng/ - content

432. 语言/yǔ yán/ - language

433. 中文/zhōng wén/ - Chinese (language)

434. 语法/yǔ fǎ/ - grammar

435. 对话/duì huà/ - dialog

436. 方面/fāng miàn/ - aspect

437. 情况/qíng kuàng/ - circumstance; situation

438. 原因/yuán yīn/ - cause; reason

439. 教育/jiào yù/ - education; to educate

450. 计划/jì huá/ - plan; to plan

451. 标准/biāo zhǔn/ - standard

452. 规定/guī dìng/ - regulation; rule; to stipulate

453. 活动/huó dòng/ - activity; to exercise; loose

你需要稍微多活动一下。- You need to exercise a bit more.

这个螺丝活动了。- This screw is loose.

454. 经历/jīng lì/ - experience; to experience

455. 实际/shí jì/ - reality; actual

456. 友谊/yǒu yì/ - friendship

457. 友情/yǒu qíng/ - friendship

458. 生活/shēng huó/ - life; to live

外国的生活方式与我们不同。- Foreign countries have a different way of life from us.

他靠正当的劳动生活。- He lives by honest labor.

459. 生命/shēng mìng/ - life

生命是怎么起源的？- How did life begin?

460. 生意/ shēng yi/ - business

461. 民族/mín zú/ - ethnic group
462. 爱情/ài qíng/ - love
463. 世纪/shì jì/ - century
464. 消息/xiāo xī/ - news; information
465. 网站/wǎng zhàn/ - website
466. 互联网/hù lián wǎng/ - the internet
467. 梦/mèng/ - dream
468. 密码/mì mǎ/ - password
469. 区别/qū bié/ - difference; to distinguish
470. 笑话/xiào huà/ - joke
471. 范围/fàn wéi/ - scope

Chapter 2. Verbs and Auxiliary Verbs

Chinese verbs do not conjugate like verbs from most Indo-European languages, such as English or Spanish. In fact, there is no strict morphological change in the Chinese language. The form of a verb remains unchanged under all circumstances. Differences in person, gender, and instances do not require changes in the form of a verb.

472. 谢谢/xiè xie/ – to thank; thanks

473. 不客气/bú kè qì/ – you're welcome; it's my pleasure

474. 再见/zài jiàn/ – goodbye

475. 请/qǐng/ – please (do something); to treat (to a meal, etc.) 他要请我看球赛。– He's going to treat me to a football match.

476. 对不起/duì bù qǐ/ – I'm sorry; excuse me; pardon me

477. 没关系/méi guān xi/ – don't worry about it

478. 欢迎/huān yíng/ – to welcome

479. 是/shì/ – be (to express judgment, existence or denote classification)

480. 有/yǒu/ – to have; there be

481. 看/kàn/ – to look at
/kān/ – to guard

有两个入口的房子很难看守。- A house with two entrances is difficult to guard.

482. 听/tīng/ - to listen; to hear; to obey; measure word for canned beverages

483. 说话/shuō huà/ - to speak; to say

484. 读/dú/ - to read; to pronounce

485. 写/xiě/ - to write

486. 看见/kàn jiàn/ - to see

487. 叫/jiào/ - to call; to shout; to order

你叫我什么？- What did you call me?

别叫了！- Stop shouting!

我给你叫辆出租车吧。- Let me order a taxi for you.

488. 来/lái/ - to come; to arrive

489. 回/huí/ - to go back; to return; measure word (for acts of a play); section or chapter (of a classical book)

490. 去/qù/ - to go; to go to (a place); to remove; to delete

请把这一段去了。- Please delete this paragraph.

491. 吃/chī/ - to eat

492. 喝/hē/ - to drink

493. 睡觉/shuì jiào/ - to go to sleep; to go to bed

494. 打电话/dǎ diàn huà/ - to make a phone call

495. 做/zuò/ - to do; to make; to produce

496. 买/mǎi/ - to buy; to purchase

497. 卖/mài/ - to sell

498. 开/fān/ - to open; to start; to turn on; to operate (vehicle, ship, plane, etc.)

499. 坐/zuò/ - to sit; to take (a bus, airplane, etc.)

500. 住/zhù/ - to live; to dwell; to stay

501. 学习/xué xí/ - to learn; to study

502. 工作/gōng zuò/ - to work; job

他在工作。- He's working now.

他需要一份工作。- He needs a job.

503. 下雨/xià yǔ/ - rain

504. 问/wèn/ - to ask

505. 走/zǒu/ - to walk; to go; to leave

506. 进/jìn/ - to enter; to go into

507. 出/chū/ - to go out; to come out; measure word (for dramas, plays, operas, etc.)

508. 赶/gǎn/ - to catch up with; to try to catch (the bus, etc.); to drive (someone/something) away; to drive (cattle, etc.) forward

我赶不上他。- I couldn't catch up with him.

他要赶末班车。- He's trying to catch the last bus.

我被她从屋里赶出来了。- She drove me out of the house.

牧羊人把羊群向前赶。- The shepherd drove the sheep forward.

509. 跑步/pǎo bù/ - to run; to take a walk

510. 到/dào/ - to (a place); until (a time); to arrive; to go

511. 穿/chuān/ - to wear; to put on

512. 洗/xǐ/ - to wash

513. 给/gěi/ - to give; to do something (for someone); for (someone); (for an imperative tone)

你能把那个盒子给我吗？- Can you give me that box?

他给我带来了圣诞礼物。- He brought me a Christmas present.

这是给她的。- This is for her.

你给我过来！- Come here, now!

514. 找/zhǎo/ - to look for; to call on someone; to find; to give change

515. 付款/fù kuǎn/ - to pay

516. 懂/dǒng/ - to understand; to know

517. 笑/xiào/ - to laugh; to smile

518. 回答/huí dá/ - to reply; to answer; answer

519. 告诉/gào sù/ - to tell; to inform

520. 准备/zhǔn bèi/ - to prepare; preparation

521. 开始/kāi shǐ/ - to begin; to start; beginning

522. 介绍/jiè shào/ - to introduce

523. 帮助/bāng zhù/ - to help; to assist; help; assistance

524. 玩/wán/ - to play

525. 送/sòng/ - to give (as a present); to see off; to send

我送了她一条项链。- I gave her a necklace.

我得去送我父母。- I have to see off my parents.

请把这些样品送北京去。- Please send these samples to Beijing.

526. 等/děng/ - to wait for; and so on; as soon as, etc.

请等我一会儿。- Please wait for me for a while.

527. 我喜欢体育运动，如打篮球、踢足球等。- I like sports; for example, basketball, soccer, and so on.

等他来了我们就能开始。- We can get started as soon as he arrives.

528. 让/ràng/ - to let someone do something; to give something willingly

让她进来吧。- Let her in.

这件外套我让给你了。- I'll give you this coat.

529. 起床/qǐ chuáng/ - to get up

530. 唱歌/chàng gē/ - to sing a song

531. 跳舞/tiào wǔ/ - to dance

532. 旅游/lǚ yóu/ - to go on a trip; travel; tour

533. 旅行/lǚ xíng/ - to travel; journey; trip

534. 上班/shàng bān/ - to go to work

535. 生病/shēng bìng/ - to fall ill

536. 休息/xiū xi/ - to rest; rest

537. 运动/yùn dòng/ - to exercise; sports

538. 游泳/yóu yǒng/ - to swim; swimming

539. 踢足球/tī zú qiú/ - to play football

540. 打篮球/dǎ lán qiú/ - to play basketball

541. 完/wán/ - to finish; to be over

542. 差/chāi/ - to assign (someone to do something)
老板差我去买烟。- The boss told me to buy cigarettes.
/chā/ - bad (student); difference (math)
他是个差生。- He's a bad student.
/chà/ - bad; wrong; poor (quality); to lack
这件外套质量很差。- The quality of this coat is poor.
这道题你做差了。- You've done wrong on this question.
他态度很差。- He has a bad attitude.
她离终点就差那么一点儿。- She only a little bit from the finish line. (She's so close to the finish line.)

543. 刮风/guā fēng/ - to be windy

544. 建议/jiàn yì/ - to suggest; to recommend; suggestion; recommendation

545. 感冒/gǎn mào/ - to catch cold

546. 发烧/fā shāo/ - to have a fever

547. 生气/shēng qì/ - to get angry

548. 哭/kū/ - to cry; to weep

549. 满意/mǎn yì/ - to be satisfied; satisfaction

550. 忘记/wàng jì/ - to forget

551. 照顾/zhào gù/ - to take care of (someone); to look after; care

552. 画/huà/ - to draw; painting

553. 带/dài/ - to carry; to bring; to take; to lead

带上这个！- Take this!

带路吧！- Lead the way!

把他带来。- Bring him to me.

你不能带这个。- You can't carry this.

554. 放/fàng/ - to set off (fire, fireworks, etc.); to release; to let go; to put; to place

555. 讲/jiǎng/ - to speak

556. 用/yòng/ - to use

557. 存/cún/ - to save; to keep; to store

558. 借/jiè/ - to borrow

559. 还/huán/ - to return (money, books, etc.)

/hái/ - still; yet

你怎么还在这儿？- Why are you still here?

我还没走。- I haven't gone yet.

560. 把/bǎ/ - to hold; measure word for chairs and objects with handles

帮我把一下门。- Please hold the door for me.

561. 拿/ná/ - to hold; to take

拿着。- Hold this.

把它拿走吧。- Just take it away.

562. 站/zhàn/ - to stand; station

563. 像/xiàng/ - to look like; to be similar to; image; portrait

564. 接/jiē/ - to answer (the phone); to pick someone up

没人接我电话。- No one answered my phone.

谢谢你来机场接我。- Thank you for picking me up from the airport.

565. 转/zhuǎn/ - to turn; to change direction; to transfer; to forward (mail, phone call)

/zhuàn/ - to spin

566. 搬/bān/ – to move

567. 倒/dào/ – to move backward

/dǎo/ – to fall

568. 花/huā/ – to spend (money, time); blossom

569. 教/jiāo/ – to teach

570. 换/huàn/ – to change; to exchange

571. 关/guān/ – to close; to shut; to turn off; mountain pass

572. 骑/qí/ – to ride

573. 复习/fù xí/ – to revise; to review; revision

574. 发现/fā xiàn/ – to find

575. 打算/dǎ suàn/ – to plan; to intend; intention; plan

你打算做什么？– What do you intend to do?

你有什么打算？– What's your plan?

576. 决定/jué dìng/ – to decide; decision

577. 认为/rèn wéi/ – to believe; to think; to consider; to feel

578. 选择/xuǎn zé/ – to choose; to select; choice

579. 表演/biǎo yǎn/ – to act; to perform; show; performance

580. 同意/tóng yì/ – to agree; to approve

581. 明白/míng bái/ – to understand; to realize

582. 了解/le jiě/ – to understand; to realize; to find out

583. 举行/jǔ xíng/ – to hold (meetings, ceremony, etc.)

584. 举办/jǔ bàn/ – to hold (events, activities, etc.)

585. 变化/biàn huà/ – to change; change

586. 提高/tí gāo/ – to improve

587. 出现/chū xiàn/ – to appear; to show up

588. 检查/jiǎn chá/ – to inspect; to examine; inspection

589. 学习/xué xí/ – to study; study

590. 研究/yán jiū/ – to research; research

591. 遇到/yù dào/ – to run into; to come across

592. 解决/jiě jué/ – to solve

593. 迟到/chí dào/ - to be late

594. 影响/yǐng xiǎng/ - to influence; to disturb; influence; effect

他正在试图影响警察的判断。- He is trying to influence the judgment of the police.

别影响我！- Don't disturb me.

我当时深受一位历史老师的影响。- I was deeply influenced by a history teacher at the time.

595. 需要/xū yào/ - to need; to want; to demand; needs

596. 注意/zhù yì/ - to pay attention to; to focus; to notice;

597. 要求/yāo qiú/ - to ask; to demand; to request; to require; requirement

598. 离开/lí kāi/ - to leave

599. 爬山/pá shān/ - to climb a mountain; to go hiking

600. 锻炼/duàn liàn/ - to exercise; exercise

601. 洗澡/xǐ zǎo/ - to take a shower

602. 参加/cān jiā/ - to participate; to join

603. 见面/jiàn miàn/ - to meet; to see someone

604. 完成/wán chéng/ - to complete; to finish; to accomplish

605. 结束/jié shù/ - to finish; to end; termination

606. 结婚/jié hūn/ - to marry; to get married

607. 表示/biǎo shì/ - to express; to indicate; to show

608. 刷牙/shuā yá/ - to brush one's teeth

609. 上网/shàng wǎng/ - to be on the internet

610. 留学/liú xué/ - to study abroad

611. 根据/gēn jù/ - to be based on; according to; basis; foundation

612. 疼/téng/ - to love; ache; sore

奶奶很疼我。- My grandmother loves me.

我头疼。- I have a headache.

我背疼。- I have a sore back.

613. 以为/yǐ wéi/ - to think; to believe

614. 打扫/dǎ sǎo/ - to clean; to sweep

615. 干/gàn/ - to do (some work)
/gān/ - dry

616. 拉/lā/ - to pull; to drag

617. 抱/bào/ - to hug; to embrace

618. 推/tuī/ - to push forward

619. 扔/rēng/ - to throw (away)

620. 挂/guà/ - to hang (from a hook, etc.); to hang up (a phone call); to be killed (colloquial); to cheat (in the game)

他刚上战场就挂了。- He was killed as soon as he went to war.

这个玩家开挂！- This player is cheating!

621. 抬/tái/ - to raise; (of two or more persons) to carry

能帮我抬一下吗？- Can you help me to carry this?

抬起头来。- Raise your head.

622. 举/jǔ/ - to raise (something overhead)

举起手来！- Raise your hands! (Hands up!)

623. 提/tí/ - to lift; to raise; to carry (in one's hand with the arm down); to mention

他提着一袋米。- He was carrying a bag of rice.

别提了。- Don't mention it.

624. 撞/zhuàng/ - to hit

625. 擦/cā/ - to wipe

626. 指/zhǐ/ - to point at; to point to; to indicate; to refer to

627. 戴/dài/ - to put on or wear (glasses, hat, gloves, etc.)

628. 尝/cháng/ - to taste

629. 躺/tǎng/ - to lie down

630. 敲/qiāo/ - to knock (at a door); to hit

631. 表扬/biǎo yáng/ - to praise; to commend

632. 道歉/dào qiàn/ - to apologize

633. 商量/shāng liàng/ – to talk over; to discuss

634. 抽烟/chōu yān/ – to smoke (a cigarette)

635. 咳嗽/ké sòu/ – to cough

636. 收拾/shōu shí/ – to tidy up; to give someone a lesson (colloquial)

我去收拾他！– I'll teach him a lesson!

637. 握手/wò shǒu/ – to shake hands

638. 鼓掌/gǔ zhǎng/ – to applaud

639. 打针/dǎ zhēn/ – to have or gave an injection

640. 值得/zhí dé/ – to be worth; to deserve

641. 逛/guàng/ – to stroll; to walk around

642. 流泪/liú lèi/ – to weep

643. 起来/qǐ lái/ – to rise; to stand up; (beginning or continuing an action)

说着说着她就哭了起来。– While talking, she began to cry.

说着说着她又哭了起来。– While talking, she cried again.

644. 散步/sàn bù/ – to take a walk; to go for a walk

645. 死/sǐ/ – to die; to be dead

646. 赢/yíng/ – to win

647. 输/shū/ – to lose; to enter (a password)

648. 断/duàn/ – to break

649. 丢/diū/ – to lose; to throw

他钱包丢了。– He lost his wallet.

麻烦你把那个帽子丢过来。– Please throw that hat over.

650. 掉/diào/ – to fall; to lose; to turn

秋天，树叶纷纷从树上掉下来。– Leaves fall off the trees in the autumn.

他钱包掉了。– He lost his wallet.

此路不通，请掉头！– This road is blocked, please turn around!

651. 增加/zēng jiā/ – to raise; to increase

652. 增长/zēng zhǎng/ - to grow

653. 减少/jiǎn shǎo/ - to reduce; to decrease

654. 通过/tōng guò/ - to pass through; to get through; by means of

你不能从这儿通过。- You're not allowed to pass through here.

通过这件事，我认识到自己的不足。- I realized my shortcomings from this incident.

655. 进行/jìn xíng/ - to carry on; in progress

会议的准备工作正在进行。- Preparations for the meeting are in progress.

我希望能进行一段时间。- I hope to carry on for an indeterminate period.

656. 继续/jì xù/ - to continue

657. 成为/chéng wéi/ - to become; to turn into

658. 提前/tí qián/ - to advance; to bring forward; in advance

659. 降低/jiàng dī/ - to lower; to reduce; to bring down

660. 降落/jiàng luò/ - to land

661. 获得/huò dé/ - to obtain

662. 接受/jiē shòu/ - to accept

663. 拒绝/jù jué/ - to refuse; to decline; to reject

664. 取/qǔ/ - to take; to get; to fetch

665. 成功/chéng gōng/ - to succeed; success

他成功当上了厂长。- He succeeded in becoming the factory manager.

失败是成功之母。- Failure is the mother of success.

666. 失败/shī bài/ - to fail; to lose; to be defeated; failure

667. 陪/péi/ - to accompany

668. 剩/shèng/ - to be left; to remain

669. 当/dāng/ - to be; when; to (do something, say something to) one's face; at (a time or place); to take responsibility

我想当科学家。- I want to be a scientist.

当我无聊的时候，我喜欢听歌。- I like listening to music when I'm bored.

你在当着我的面撒谎。- You are telling me lies to my face.

你当时怎么做的？- What did you do at that time?

一人做事一人当。- One should take responsibility for their actions.

/dàng/ - to think; to pawn; that very (day, etc.); to treat as; to take for

我当是她呢。- I thought it was her.

他把表当了。- He pawned his watch.

他父亲突然病重，当月就过世了。- His father suddenly got seriously ill and died that month.

不要把我当小孩看。- Don't treat me like a child.

670. 寄/jì/ - to send; to mail

671. 修/xiū/ - to fix; to repair

672. 修理/xiū lǐ/ - to repair; to fix; to teach someone a lesson (colloquial)

673. 弄/nòng/ - to play with; to make someone do something; to do; to get someone or something into a specified condition; to get

别弄我的头发。- Don't play with my hair.

别把孩子弄哭了。- Don't make the child cry.

弄得不好，就会前功尽弃。- If we don't do a good job now, all the work we've done will be wasted.

他把衣服弄脏了。- He got his clothes dirty.

你去弄点水来。- Go and get some water.

674. 养成/yǎng chéng/ - to cultivate

675. 过/guò/ - to cross; to pass; to spend (time); after; to undergo a process; over; to exceed; past; to live; to celebrate; excessively; demerit

过街时注意车辆。- When crossing the street, watch out for cars.

假期过得怎么样？- How did you spend your holiday?

过了夏至，天就开始变短。- The days get shorter after the summer solstice.

我们再过一遍这篇稿子。- Let's go over the draft once again.

他已经年过70了。- He's over 70 years old.

小鹿跳过篱笆墙。- The deer jumped over a fence.

小心别坐过了站。- Be sure you don't go past your station.

她过得很开心。- She lives a happy life.

我们明天给他过生日。- We will celebrate his birthday tomorrow.

他已被记过三次。- He already has three demerits on his record.

这位经理还被指责给自己支付过高的薪水。- This manager is also accused of paying himself an excessively high salary.

676. 留/liú/ - to stay; to keep; to leave; to remain

677. 试/shì/ - to try; to test

678. 脱/tuō/ - to take off

679. 赚/zhuàn/ - to earn; to make a profit

680. 租/zū/ - to rent

681. 填空/tián kòng/ - to fill in a blank

682. 发/fā/ - to send out; measure word for gunshots

683. 骗/piàn/ - to cheat; to deceive; to fool

684. 猜/cāi/ - to guess

685. 发生/fā shēng/ - to happen; to take place; to occur

686. 引起/yǐn qǐ/ - to lead to; to cause

687. 使用/shǐ yòng/ - to use

688. 管理/guǎn lǐ/ - to manage; to supervise; management; administration

689. 批评/pī píng/ - to criticize; criticism

690. 适合/shì hé/ - to fit; to suit; suitable

绿色很适合你。- Green suits you.

我找不到适合的衣服。- I can't find clothes that fit me.

她没有其他适合这种场合穿的套裙。- She had no other dress suitable for the occasion.

691. 适应/shì yīng/ - to fit; to adapt; to get used to something

他过去从未干过这种工作，我不确定他能适应。- He's never done this type of work before; I'm not sure how he'll fit in.

这些样式可以修改，以适应个人不同爱好。- These styles can be adapted to suit individual tastes.

692. 吸引/xī yǐn/ - to attract

693. 提供/tí gōng/ - to provide; to offer

694. 交流/jiāo liú/ - to communicate; communication

695. 表达/biǎo dá/ - to express

696. 算/suàn/ - to calculate

697. 浪费/làng fèi/ - to waste

698. 保护/bǎo hù/ - to protect; to defend; protection

699. 代表/dài biǎo/ - to represent; representative

700. 安排/ān pái/ - to arrange

701. 反映/fǎn yìng/ - to reflect; reflex

他们的行动清楚地反映了他们的思想。- Their actions clearly reflect their thoughts.

法律应该是人民意志的反映。- The law should represent the will of the people.

702. 讨论/tǎo lùn/ - to discuss

703. 改变/gǎi biàn/ - to change; to alter

704. 超过/chāo guò/ - to surpass; to exceed

705. 放弃/fàng qì/ - to give up

706. 调查/diào chá/ - to investigate; investigation

707. 照/zhào/ - to shine; to look in the mirror; to take (photo); as (requested, etc.)

他用手电筒往地窖各处照了照。- He shone the flashlight around the cellar.

我照了照镜子，看见自己满脸是汗。- I looked in the mirror and saw that my face was covered in sweat.

能不能帮我照张像？- Could you please take a photo for me?

照我说的做。- Do as I say.

708. 联系/lián xì/ - to link; to contact; contact; connection

709. 停/tíng/ - to stop; to halt; to park (a car)

710. 停止/tíng zhǐ/ - to stop

711. 缺少/quē shǎo/ - to lack; to be short of

712. 通知/tōng zhī/ - to notify; to inform; notice; notification

713. 翻译/fān yì/ - to translate; translator; translation

714. 组织/zǔ zhī/ - to organize; organization

715. 发展/fā zhǎn/ - to develop; development

716. 阅读/yuè dú/ - to read; reading

717. 鼓励/gǔ lì/ - to encourage

718. 预习/yù xí/ - to prepare a lesson

719. 访问/fǎng wèn/ - to visit; to interview; visit

720. 信任/xìn rèn/ - to trust; to believe in

721. 坚持/jiān chí/ - to insist on; to persist; persistence

722. 受到/shòu dào/ - to suffer

723. 重视/zhòng shì/ - to attach importance to something; to value

724. 复印/fù yìn/ - to photocopy

725. 打印/dǎ yìn/ - to print

726. 打扰/dǎ rǎo/ - to disturb; to bother; to interrupt; to trouble

727. 打招呼/dǎ zhāo hu/ - to greet someone
728. 扩大/kuò dà/ - to expand; expansion
729. 整理/zhěng lǐ/ - to collate (data; files); to tidy up; to sort out
730. 组成/zǔ chéng/ - to consist of
731. 参观/cān guān/ - to look around
732. 集合/jí hé/ - to gather
733. 总结/zǒng jié/ - to sum up; to conclude; summary
734. 节约/jiē yuē/ - to economize; to conserve (resources)
735. 放松/fàng sōng/ - to relax
736. 限制/xiàn zhì/ - to restrict; to restrain; restriction
737. 请假/qǐng jià/ - to ask for time off
738. 放暑假/fàng shǔ jià/ - to take a summer vacation
739. 负责/fù zé/ - to be responsible for; to take responsibility for
740. 证明/zhèng míng/ - to prove; to testify; proof
741. 广播/guǎng bō/ - to broadcast; broadcast
742. 保证/bǎo zhèng/ - to guarantee; to ensure; guarantee
743. 代替/dài tì/ - to replace
744. 毕业/bì yè/ - to graduate; graduation
745. 请客/qǐng kè/ - treat
今天我请客。- I'm treating (you) today. (It's on me today.)
746. 申请/shēn qǐng/ - to apply; application
747. 出发/chū fā/ - to set off; to start out
748. 污染/wū rǎn/ - pollution; to contaminate
749. 出差/chū chāi/ - to go on a business trip
750. 报名/bào míng/ - to sign up
751. 约会/yuē huì/ - appointment; date
752. 邀请/yāo qǐng/ - to invite; invitation
753. 理发/lǐ fā/ - to get a haircut
754. 估计/gū jì/ - to estimate
755. 解释/jiě shì/ - to explain; explanation

756. 说明/shuō míng/ - to explain; to illustrate; instruction

757. 理解/lǐ jiě/ - to comprehend; to understand; comprehension; understanding

758. 聊天/liáo tiān/ - to chat

759. 竞争/jìng zhēng/ - to compete; competition

760. 打折/dǎ zhé/ - to give a discount

761. 打扮/dǎ bàn/ - to dress up; manner of dressing

762. 招聘/zhāo pìn/ - to invite applications for a job; recruitment

763. 出生/chū shēng/ - to be born

764. 制造/zhì zào/ - to manufacture

765. 包括/bāo kuò/ - to include

766. 符合 /fú hé/ - in accordance with; to agree with; to correspond with; to conform to

767. 行/xíng/ - to do; to perform; all right; OK; acceptable
这个方案简单易行。 - This plan is simple and easy to perform.
行，就这么定了。 - OK, it's settled.
她教英语行吗？ - Is she competent at teaching English?
/háng/ - line; row
请站成一行。 - Please stand in one row.
我对此不打在行。 - That's not much in my line.

768. 例如/lì rú/ - such as; for example; for instance; e.g.

769. 受不了/shòu bu liǎo/ - can't stand; unbearable

770. 做生意 zuò shēng yì/ - to do business

771. 弹钢琴/tán gāng qín/ - to play the piano

772. 开玩笑/kāi wán xiào/ - to joke

773. 醒/xǐng/ - to wake up; to awaken; to be awake

774. 响/xiǎng/ - to make a sound; to sound; loud

775. 积累/jī lèi/ - to accumulate; accumulation

776. 禁止/jìn zhǐ/ - to prohibit; to forbid; to ban

777. 推迟/tuī chí/ - to postpone; to put off

778. 干杯/gān bēi/ – Cheers! (proposing a toast); Bottoms up!

779. 祝贺/zhù hè/ – to congratulate; congratulations

780. 回忆/huí yì/ – to recall; recollection

781. 免费/miǎn fèi/ – free (of charge)

782. 谈/tán/ – to talk

783. 提醒/tí xǐng/ – to remind

784. 来不及/lái bù jí/ – there's not enough time (to do something); it's too late (to do something)

785. 来得及/lái de jí/ – there's still time; able to do something in time

786. 误会/wù huì/ – to misunderstand; misunderstanding

787. 同情/tóng qíng/ – to show sympathy for; to sympathize; compassion

788. 不得不/bù dé bù/ – have to

我不得不走了。– I have to go.

789. 加班/jiā bān/ – to work overtime

790. 帮忙/bāng máng/ – to help; to do a favor

791. 乘坐/chéng zuò/ – to ride (in a vehicle, train, plane, ship, etc.)

792. 购物/gòu wù/ – to go shopping

793. 起飞/qǐ fēi/ – to take off

794. 收/shōu/ – to receive; to collect

795. 减肥/jiǎn féi/ – to lose weight

796. 交/jiāo/ – to hand over; to make (friends); to pay (money)

797. 允许/yǔn xǔ/ – to permit; to allow; permission

798. 判断/pàn duàn/ – to judge; judgment

799. 排列/pái liè/ – to line; to rank; permutation

800. 爱/ài/ – to love; love

801. 喜欢/xǐ huān/ – to like

802. 想/xiǎng/ – to think; to wish; to want; to miss

我想我得走了。– I think I need to go.

我想有个假期。– I want to go on holiday.

他想去博物馆。– He wants to go to the museum.

她想家了。– She misses her home. (She is homesick.)

803. 认识/rèn shi/ – to know; to realize; to understand.

我认识这个地方。– I know this place.

他已经认识到自己的过错了。– He has realized the mistakes he made.

请谈谈你对这件事的认识。– Please talk about your understanding of this matter.

804. 觉得/jué de/ – to think; to feel

805. 知道/zhī dào/ – to know; to be aware of

806. 希望/xī wàng/ – to wish; to hope; hope

我希望我能做那件事。– I wish I could do that.

我希望你会成为我们的靠山。– I hope that you will become our patron.

有生命就有希望。– Where there is life, there is hope.

807. 祝/zhù/ – to wish; to hope

祝你成功！– (I) wish you success!

祝你健康！– (I) hope you are well!

808. 关心/guān xīn/ – to care; to be concerned

809. 担心/dān xīn/ – to worry; to be worried

810. 烦恼/fán nǎo/ – to worry; trouble

不要为小事烦恼。– Don't worry over trifles.

有什么事情让你烦恼吗？– Is anything troubling you?

咱们忘掉那些烦恼吧。– Let's forget about those troubles.

811. 放心/fàng xīn/ – to be at ease; to set one's mind at rest

812. 小心/xiǎo xīn/ – to be careful; to watch out

813. 害怕/hài pà/ – to be afraid; to be scared

814. 相信/xiàng xìn/ - to believe

815. 记得/jì dé/ - to remember

816. 努力/nǔ lì/ - to try hard; to make great effort

817. 使/shǐ/ - to use; to make

我能使一下你的笔吗？- May I use your pen for a while?

什么使你这么想呢？- What makes you think so?

818. 讨厌/tǎo yàn/ - to dislike; to hate; annoying

819. 后悔/hòu huǐ/ - to regret

820. 失望/shī wàng/ - to despair; disappointed

821. 羡慕/xiàn mù/ - to admire; to envy

822. 怀疑/huái yí/ - to suspect; to doubt; suspicion

823. 感谢/gǎn xiè/ - (to express) thanks; gratitude

非常感谢你能加入。- Thank you for joining us.

824. 原谅/yuán liàng/ - to forgive; to excuse; to pardon; forgiveness

825. 支持/zhī chí/ - to support; to stand by; support

826. 尊重/zūn zhòng/ - to honor; to respect; respect

827. 反对/fǎn duì/ - to fight against; to oppose; opposition

828. 考虑/kǎo lǜ/ - to think over; consideration

Auxiliary verbs occur before a verb and express the meanings of possibility, ability, permission, obligation, and prohibition.

829. 会/huì/ - can; to be able to; will; to meet; meeting; a moment

我会说中文。- I can speak Chinese.

我会骑马。- I'm able to ride a horse.

他会来吗？- Will he come?

830. 她要到公园会男朋友。- She's going to the party to meet her boyfriend.

今下午有个会要开。- I have a meeting to attend in the afternoon.

我一会就来。- I'll come in a moment.

158

831. 能/néng/ - can; to be able to; to be capable of

我能自己去。- I can go by myself.

你明天能来吗？- Are you able to come tomorrow?

我自己能行。- I'm capable of doing it alone.

832. 可以/kě yǐ/ - can; may

我们可以帮助你。- We can help you.

我可以抽烟吗？- May I smoke a cigarette here?

833. 要/yào/ - need; be going to; to want; to take

你要好好学习。- You need to study hard.

天要下雨。- It's going to rain.

我要回家。- I want to go home.

我要了。- I'll take it.

834. 可能/kě néng/ - might; maybe; possible; possibly; possibility

我以为你可能已经邀请他过来了。- I thought you might have invited him over.

我可能错了。- Maybe I was wrong.

有可能。- It's possible.

我不可能放弃工作。- I couldn't possibly give up work.

我的确想过有失败的可能。- The possibility of failure did cross my mind.

835. 应该/yīng gāi/ - should; ought to

836. 愿意/yuàn yì/ - will; to be willing to

你愿意和我换一下座位吗？- Will you change seats with me?

他很愿意找我的要价付钱。- He's quite willing to pay the price I ask.

837. 敢/gǎn/ - to dare

他们怎么敢做出这样的事？- How dare they do such a thing?

Chapter 3. Pronouns and Adjectives

Chinese pronouns are not distinguished in terms of grammatical roles. The same pronouns are used for subject, object, possession, etc. Some pronouns have singular and plural forms. The suffix –们 /men/ is added to the singular form to turn it into the plural form. In addition, gender is not reflected in the spoken language. The written language has distinctions for second- and third-person pronouns, though only the third-person gender distinction is commonly used.

838. 我/wǒ/ – I; me

839. 你/nǐ/ – you (singular; informal)

840. 您/nín/ – you (singular; formal)

841. 他/tā/ – he; him; (used for either sex when the sex is unknown or unimportant)

842. 她/tā/ – she; her

843. 它/tā/ – it

844. 我们/wǒ men/ – we; us

845. 咱们/zán men/ – we; us (colloquial)

846. 这(这儿)/zhè (zhèr)/ – this; those; here

847. 那(那儿)/nà (nàer)/ – that; those; there

848. 哪(哪儿)/nǎ (nǎer)/ – where; which

849. 谁/shuí/ – who; whom

850. 什么/shén me/ – what

851. 多少/duō shǎo/ – how much; how many
桌子上有多少个苹果？– How many apples are on the table?
你还有多少钱？– How much money do you have?

852. 几/jǐ/ – how much; how many; several; a few
我几天前来的。– I came here several days ago.
我就呆几天。– I just stay for a few days.

853. 怎么/zěn me/ – how

854. 怎么样/zěn me yàng/ – how about; what about

855. 大家/dà jiā/ – everyone

856. 为什么/wèi shén me/ – why

857. 自己/zì jǐ/ – self; own

858. 别人/bié rén/ – other people

859. 其他/qí tā/ – other; else

860. 一切/yí qiè/ – everything; all

861. 任何/rèn hé/ – whatever; whichever; whatsoever

862. 每/měi/ – every; each

863. 各/gè/ – each; every

Adjectives describe the shape or property of a person or thing or the state of a movement or action. In Chinese, the form of an adjective remains unchanged in all circumstances.

864. 好/hǎo/ – good; well; fine; very; easy to
我很好。– I'm fine.
我好高兴。– I'm very happy.
她是一个好相处的人。– She's easy to get along with.

865. 大/dà/ – big; huge; large; old
我喜欢住大房子。– I like to live in a big house.
她比我大两岁。– She is two years older than me.

866. 小/xiǎo/ - small; tiny; young

这双鞋子太小了。- This pair of shoes is too small.

我比她小三岁。- I'm three years younger than her.

867. 多/duō/ - a lot of; more; many; much

我的积蓄不多了。- I don't have many savings.

他的收入比我多。- He earns more than me.

868. 少/shǎo/ - few; little

869. 冷/lěng/ - cold

870. 热/rè/ - hot (of weather); to heat

今天真热。- What a hot day today.

请帮我把鸡汤热一下。- Please heat up the chicken soup for me.

871. 高兴/gāo xìng/ - happy; glad; willing (to do something)

872. 漂亮/piào liàng/ - beautiful; pretty

873. 高/gāo/ - high; tall; Gao (surname)

874. 红/hóng/ - red

875. 白/bái/ - white; Bai (surname)

876. 黑/hēi/ - black; dark

877. 忙/máng/ - busy

878. 快/kuài/ - fast; quick; sharp (of knives or wits)

879. 慢/màn/ - slow

880. 远/yuǎn/ - far

881. 近/jìn/ - near; close to

882. 好吃/hǎo chī/ - tasty; delicious

883. 累/lèi/ - tired

884. 长/cháng/ - long; length

它脖子很长。- Its neck is long.

它长约一米。- It's about a meter in length.

/zhǎng/ - to grow

这孩子一年不见，长这么高了。- It's only a year since I saw the child last time and he's grown so tall.

885. 新/xīn/ - new

886. 贵/guì/ - expensive

887. 便宜/pián yi/ - cheap; inexpensive

888. 晴/qíng/ - fine (weather); sunny

889. 阴/yīn/ - cloudy; Yin (of Yin and Yang); negative (electric)

890. 错/cuò/ - wrong; fault

我错了。- I was wrong.

这是我的错。- It's my fault.

891. 快乐/kuài lè/ - happy

892. 蓝/lán/ - blue

893. 绿/lǜ/ - green

894. 黄/huáng/ - yellow; Huang (surname)

895. 低/dī/ - low; beneath; too low

896. 矮/ǎi/ - low; short (in height)

897. 短/duǎn/ - short (in length)

898. 久/jiǔ/ - (long) time; (long) duration of time

899. 旧/jiù/ - old (of things); worn (with age)

900. 老/lǎo/ - old (of people); tough (of meat, etc.)

901. 容易/róng yì/ - easy

902. 难/nán/ - difficult

/nàn/ - disaster

903. 坏/huài/ - bad; broken; to break down

904. 甜/tián/ - sweet

905. 饱/bǎo/ - to be full

906. 空/kōng/ - empty; vacant
/kòng/ - space; to be free
你有空吗？- Are you free?
仓库里还有空吗？- Is there any space in the warehouse?

907. 相同/xiàng tóng/ - same; identical

908. 简单/jiǎn dān/ - simple; easy

909. 一样/yí yàng/ - the same as; same; just like; equal to

910. 有名/yǒu míng/ - famous; well known

911. 重要/zhòng yào/ - important; significant

912. 全部/quán bù/ - whole; entire

913. 一般/yì bān/ - ordinary; common; generally; in general

914. 清楚/qīng chǔ/ - clear; distinct; clearly; to be clear about

915. 安静/ān jìng/ - quiet

916. 方便/fāng biàn/ - convenient; to help out (to make things easy for people); (euphemism) to go to the toilet
在你方便的时候请联系我。- Please contact me when it is convenient for you.
能不能行个方便？- Could you please help me out?
我需要去方便一下。- I need to go to the toilet.

917. 干净/gàn jìng/ - clean

918. 新鲜/xīn xiān/ - fresh (air, fruit, etc.)

919. 奇怪/qí guài/ - strange; odd

920. 胖/pàng/ - fat

921. 瘦/shòu/ - tight; thin
这件裤子太瘦了。- The pants are tight.
她很瘦。- She's thin.

922. 舒服/shū fu/ - comfortable

923. 健康/jiàn kāng/ - healthy; health

924. 饿/è/ - hungry

925. 渴/kě/ - thirsty

926. 年轻/nián qīng/ - young

927. 聪明/cōng míng/ - intelligent; smart

928. 可爱/kě ài/ - cute; lovely

929. 认真/rèn zhēn/ - conscientious; earnest; to take seriously

930. 热情/rè qíng/ - enthusiastic; passionate; passion; passionately

931. 难过/nán guò/ - sad; upset

932. 着急/zhe jí/ - anxious; to worry

933. 紧张/jǐn zhāng/ - nervous

934. 突然/tū rán/ - sudden; suddenly

935. 主要/zhǔ yào/ - main; major

936. 合适/hé shì/ - suitable; to fit

937. 假/jiǎ/ - fake

938. 富/fù/ - rich

939. 穷/qióng/ - poor

940. 轻/qīng/ - light (of weight); gentle; soft

941. 重/zhòng/ - heavy

942. 宽/kuān/ - wide; broad

943. 窄/zhǎi/ - narrow

944. 粗心/cū xīn/ - careless; thoughtless

945. 干燥/gàn zào/ - dry

946. 湿润/shī rùn/ - moist

947. 深/shēn/ - deep; dark (of color, water, etc.); late (of night)

948. 硬/yìng/ - tough; hard

他的心肠一定很硬。- His heart must be very hard.

那牛排硬得他没法吃。- The steak was so tough that he couldn't eat it.

949. 软/ruǎn/ - soft

950. 苦/kǔ/ - bitter

951. 咸/xián/ - salty

952. 酸/suān/ - sour

953. 辣/là/ - spicy

954. 暗/àn/ - dark; dim

955. 亮/liàng/ - bright

956. 安全/ān quán/ - safe; secure

957. 危险/wēi xiǎn/ - dangerous; danger

958. 暖和/nuǎn huo/ - warm

959. 凉快/liáng kuài/ - cool

960. 美丽/měi lì/ - beautiful

961. 整齐/zhěng qí/ - neat; in good order

962. 乱/luàn/ - disordered; in a mess

963. 脏/zāng/ - dirty

964. 帅/shuài/ - handsome

965. 圆/yuán/ - round; circular; circle

966. 棒/bàng/ - smart; amazing; strong (of body); rod

你真棒！- You're smart.

太棒了！- That's wonderful!

他的身体很棒。- His body is strong.

967. 紧张/jǐn zhāng/ - nervous

968. 轻松/qīng sōng/ - relaxed; relaxing

969. 冷静/lěng jìng/ - calm

970. 幸福/xìng fú/ - happiness; wellbeing

971. 愉快/yú kuài/ - delighted; pleasing; delightful

972. 感兴趣/gǎn xìng qù/ - to be interested

973. 兴奋/xīng fèn/ - exciting; excited

974. 吃惊/chī jīng/ - to be shocked

975. 可惜/kě xī/ - it is a pity; what a pity

976. 困/kùn/ - to be trapped; to be sleepy

977. 笨/bèn/ - stupid; foolish; silly

978. 诚实/chéng shí/ - honest; honesty

979. 勇敢/yǒng gǎn/ - brave

980. 优秀/yōu xiù/ – outstanding; excellent

981. 骄傲/jiāo ào/ – proud

982. 害羞/hài xiū/ – shy

983. 激动/jī dòng/ – exciting; excited

984. 感动/gǎn dòng/ – moving; to move (someone); to touch (someone emotionally)

这是一个感人的故事。– This is a moving story.

她被他的真心感动了。– She was moved by his sincerity.

985. 活泼/huó pō/ – active; lively

986. 懒/lǎn/ – lazy

987. 辛苦/xīn kǔ/ – exhausting; exhausted

988. 成熟/chéng shú/ – mature

989. 热闹/rè nao/ – bustling (with noise and excitement)

990. 孤单/gū dān/ – alone; lonely

991. 吵/chǎo/ – noisy; to argue; to disturb by making noise

你好吵！– You are so noisy!

别吵了！– Stop arguing!

别吵我！– Don't disturb me!

992. 耐心/nài xīn/ – to be patient; patience

993. 仔细/zǐ xì/ – careful; cautious

994. 友好/yǒu hǎo/ – friendly

995. 可怜/kě lián/ – pathetic; to pity

不要可怜死者。可怜活人，尤其是那些生活中没有爱的人。– Do not pity the dead. Pity the living, and above all, those who live without love.

996. 严重/yán zhòng/ – serious; severe

997. 无聊/wú liáo/ – bored; boring

998. 香/xiāng/ – fragrant; aromatic

999. 严格/yán gé/ – strict

1000. 故意/gù yì/ – to be on purpose; deliberately

1001. 随便 /suí biàn/ - casual; as one wishes

1002. 精彩 /jīng cǎi/ - splendid

1003. 复杂 /fù zá/ - complex; complicated

1004. 详细 /xiáng xì/ - detailed; in detail

1005. 丰富 /fēng fù/ - abundant

1006. 流利 /liú lì/ - fluent

1007. 有趣 /yǒu qù/ - interesting; interested

1008. 麻烦 /má fan/ - inconvenient; trouble; to trouble or bother someone

这是一件麻烦事。 - This is an inconvenient thing.

你给我们造成了很多麻烦。 - You've caused us a lot of trouble.

不好意思麻烦你。 - Sorry to bother you.

1009. 肯定 /kěn dìng/ - to confirm; to be sure; to be certain; sure; certain; affirmative

1010. 流行 /liú xíng/ - popular; to rage (of contagious disease)

1011. 直接 /zhí jiē/ - direct; directly

1012. 许多 /xǔ duō/ - a great deal of; many; much; a lot of

1013. 满 /mǎn/ - full; fill; to reach the limit; to fill; surname

他满脑子荒唐想法。 - His head is full of nonsense.

再给你满上一杯。 - Let me fill your glass once more.

缸里盛满了酒。 - The crock is filled with wine.

1014. 完全 /wán quán/ - whole; complete; totally; entirely

1015. 所有 /suǒ yǒu/ - all; to possess; to own

1016. 普遍 /pǔ biàn/ - widespread

1017. 厉害 /lì hài/ - awesome; terrible; ferocious

1018. 准确 /zhǔn què/ - accurate; exact; precise

1019. 著名 /zhù míng/ - famous; well known

1020. 正好 /zhèng hǎo/ - just (in time); just right; just enough

1021. 够 /gòu/ - to be enough

1022. 差不多 /chà bu duō/ - almost; nearly; more or less

1023. 及时/jí shí/ - in time; promptly; timely

1024. 准时/zhǔn shí/ - on time

1025. 专门/zhuān mén/ - specialized

1026. 正式/zhèng shì/ - formal; official

1027. 合格/hé gé/ - qualified

1028. 正确/zhèng què/ - correct

1029. 对/duì/ - right; correct; towards

你是对的。- You are right.

她热情地对我们伸出双手。- She warmly extended her hands towards us.

1030. 真正/zhēn zhèng/ - real; genuine; genuinely

1031. 高级/gāo jí/ - fancy

1032. 正常/zhèng cháng/ - normal

1033. 原来/yuán lái/ - original; originally; to turn out

原来是你！- It was you!

1034. 永远/yǒng yuǎn/ - forever; eternal; eternity

1035. 暂时/zàn shí/ - temporary; temporarily

1036. 相反/xiàng fǎn/ - opposite; contrary

1037. 熟悉/shú xī/ - to be familiar with; to know well

1038. 破/pò/ - worn out; to be broken; to be damaged

1039. 马虎/mǎ hu/ - careless

1040. 另外/lìng wài/ - additional; in addition; furthermore

1041. 难受/nán shòu/ - to feel unwell; to feel ill

1042. 伤心/shāng xīn/ - sad; to feel deeply hurt

1043. 积极/jī jí/ - proactive; positive; vigorous

1044. 共同/gòng tóng/ - common; together; jointly

1045. 浪漫/làng màn/ - romantic

1046. 得意/dé yì/ - to be proud or pleased of oneself

1047. 现代/xiàn dài/ - modern

1048. 幽默/yōu mò/ - humorous; humor

1049. 本来/běn lái/ - original; originally

Chapter 4. Numerals and Measure Words

1050. 零/líng/ - zero

1051. 一/yī/ - one

1052. 二/èr/ - two

1053. 三/sān/ - three

1054. 四/sì/ - four

1055. 五/wǔ/ - five

1056. 六/liù/ - six

1057. 七/qī/ - seven

1058. 八/bā/ - eight

1059. 九/jiǔ/ - nine

1060. 十/shí/ - ten

1061. 百/bǎi/ - hundred; Bai (surname)

1062. 千/qiān/ - thousand

1063. 万/wàn/ - ten thousand;

1064. 亿/yì/ - hundred million

1065. 两/liǎng/ - two (quantities); both; weight equal to 50 grams

1066. 俩/liǎ/ - two (quantities, colloquial); both (colloquial)

1067. 半/bàn/ - half

In English, mass nouns such as "coffee", "rice", and "sand" occur with measure words. In Chinese, all nouns occur with measure words when they are preceded by a specifier and/or number. Therefore, it is imperative when learning Chinese to learn every noun with its matching measure word.

1068. 个/gè/ - measure word for people or objects in general

1069. 岁/suì/ - measure word for years of age

1070. 本/běn/ - measure word for books, periodicals, files, etc.

1071. 些/xiē/ - measure word for people or objects in general; some; few; several

1072. 块/kuài/ - measure word for pieces of cloth, cake, etc.; *yuan* (colloquial)

1073. 次/cì/ - measure word for enumerated events; time; (inferior quality)

下次见！- See you next time!

这件衬衫很次。- The quality of this shirt is poor.

1074. 公斤/gōng jīn/ - kilogram (measure unit)

1075. 元/yuán/ - *yuan* (monetary unit); Yuan (surname)

1076. 件/jiàn/ - measure word for events, things, clothes, etc.

1077. 张/zhāng/ - measure word for flat objects, sheet, votes, etc.; Zhang (surname)

1078. 角/jiǎo/ - 10 cents (monetary unit); horn; angle; corner

1079. 分/fēn/ - cent (monetary unit); minute (time unit); score (in sports or games)

1080. 条/tiáo/ - measure word for long, thin things (ribbon, river, road, pants, etc.); clause (of law or treaty); strip

1081. 位/wèi/ - measure word for binary bits, customers, members, etc.

1082. 双/shuāng/ - measure word for socks, shoes, chopsticks, etc.; pair; double; two

1083. 辆/liàng/ – measure word for vehicles

1084. 层/céng/ – layer; floor (of a building); measure word for layers

1085. 座/zuò/ – measure word for buildings, mountains, etc.; seat

1086. 台/tái/ – measure word for vehicles, machines, etc.; broadcasting station

1087. 份/fèn/ – measure word for gifts, newspapers, magazines, papers, reports, contracts, etc.; share; copy;

1089. 篇/piān/ – measure word for written items

1090. 朵/duǒ/ – measure word for flowers

1091. 棵/kē/ – measure word for trees, cabbages, plants, etc.

1092. 公里/gōng lǐ/ – kilometer (measure unit)

1093. 场/chǎng/ – measure word for races, matches, activities, exams, etc.; a ground where ball games are played

1094. 群/qún/ – a group of

1095. 趟/tàng/ – measure word for trips, runs made, etc.

Chapter 5. Adverbs, Prepositions, and Conjunctions

Adverbs are generally used in front of a verb or an adjective to express time, degree, scope, repetition, negation, possibility or tone of speech, etc. Adverbs add many different kinds of meaning to a sentence.

1096. 不/bù/ - not (negative prefix); no
中文语法并不难。- Chinese grammar isn't hard.
你喜欢这个吗？不。- Do you like this? No.

1097. 很/hěn/ - very; quite

1098. 太/tài/ - too (much, many); very; extremely

1099. 都/dōu/ - all; both; already; even
所有人都过来。- All of you, come here.
我们两个都去过北京。- Both of us have been to Beijing.
我都走了！- I have already gone!
你都没去！- You didn't even go there!

1100. 别/bié/ - do not; must not; to pin
别动！- Don't move.
她在头发上别了一支鲜花。- She pinned a flower to her hair.

1101. 非常/fēi cháng/ - very; extreme

1102. 也/yě/ - also; too

1103. 最/zuì/ - most; the most

1104. 左右/zuǒ yòu/ - approximately; about; left and right; to be controlled

1105. 正在/zhèng zài/ - in the process of (doing something or happening)

他正在睡觉。- He is sleeping.

1106. 已经/yǐ jīng/ - already

1107. 一起/yī qǐ/ - together; in the same place; with; altogether

1108. 再/zài/ - once more; again

欢迎下次再来。- You're welcome back again.

1109. 又/yòu/ - again

1110. 只有/zhǐ yǒu/...才/cái/... - only if... then...

1111. 更/gèng/ - more; even more

1112. 越/yuè/ - the more...

1113. 特别/tè bié/ - especially; special; particular

1114. 比较/bǐ jiào/ - rather; comparatively; to compare

1115. 比如/bǐ rú/ - such as; for example; for instance; e.g.

1116. 一直/yì zhí/ - straight; continuously; always

1117. 总是/zǒng shì/ - always

1118. 经常/jīng cháng/ - often; regularly

1119. 终于/zhōng yú/ - at last; in the end; finally; eventually

1120. 当然/dāng rán/ - of course; certainly; absolutely

1121. 其实/qí shí/ - actually; in fact

1122. 几乎/jǐ hū/ - almost; nearly

1123. 一定/yí dìng/ - surely; certainly; must

1124. 多么/duō me/ - how (wonderful, etc.); what (a great idea, etc.); however (difficult it is, etc.)

天空是多么晴朗！- How clear the sky is!

多么奇妙的点子！- What an amazing thought!

无论多么困难，我都要坚持下去。- No matter how difficult it is, I will stick with it to the end.

1125. 马上/mǎ shàng/ - immediately; right away; at once

1126. 必须/bì xū/ - must; have to; compulsory

1127. 十分/shí fèn/ - very; extremely; ten points

1128. 尤其/yóu qí/ - especially; particularly

1129. 挺/tǐng/ - quite; to straighten up; very; to stand up for; measure word for machine guns

我今天过得挺开行。- I'm quite happy today.

我叫他们挺起身子来。- I told them to straighten up.

我挺你！- I stand up for you!

1130. 大概/dà gài/ -- roughly; probably; rough; approximate; about

1131. 大约/dà yuē/ - approximately; about

1132. 也许/yě xǔ/ - perhaps; maybe; probably

1133. 恐怕/kǒng pà/ - perhaps; maybe; to be afraid that

1134. 难道/nán dào/ - could it be said that

1135. 只好/zhī hǎo/ - without any better option; to have to; to be forced to

1136. 最好/zuì hǎo/ - best; had better

1137. 仍然/réng rán/ - still; yet

1138. 竟然/jìng rán/ - unexpectedly

1139. 到底/dào dǐ/ - finally; in the end; when all is said and done; after all; to the last

1140. 却/què/ - but; however; yet

1141. 首先/shǒu xiān/ - first of all; in the first place

1142. 其次/qí cì/ – next; secondly

1143. 最后/zuì hòu/ – finally; last; final

1144. 刚/gāng/ – just; barely

1145. 忽然/hū rán/ – suddenly

1146. 连/lián/ – to link; to connect; even; company (military)

1147. 从来/cóng lái/ – always; at all time; never (if used in a negative sentence)

他从来都是一个人吃午饭。– He always ate lunch alone.

我从来不去公厕。– I never go to the public toilet.

1148. 按时/àn shí/ – on time; on schedule

1149. 重新/chóng xīn/ – again; once more

你需要重新开始。– You need to start again.

他重新讲了一遍。– He explained it once more.

1150. 至少/zhì shǎo/ – at least

1151. 到处/dào chù/ – in all places; everywhere

1152. 互相/hù xiàng/ – each other

1153. 顺便/shùn biàn/ – without extra effort

1154. 确实/què shí/ – indeed; really

1155. 偶尔/ǒu ěr/ – occasionally; once in a while

1156. 究竟/jiū jìng/ – after all (when all is said and done)

1157. 稍微/shāo wēi/ – a little bit

1158. 甚至/shèn zhì/ – so much so that; even

1159. 往往/wǎng wǎng/ – often; frequently

Conjunctions are words that join phrases belonging to the same grammatical category and indicate a relationship like coordination, causality, condition, supposition, etc.

1160. 和/hé/ – and; with

1161. 因为/yīn wéi/ – because

1162. 所以/suǒ yǐ/ – so; therefore

1163. 但是/dàn shì/ – but; however

1164. 虽然/suī rán/ - although, though

1165. 然后/rán hòu/ - then; after that

1166. 如果/rú guǒ/ - if; in case; in the event that

1167. 一边/yì biān/ - on the one hand; one side

1168. 或者/huò zhě/ - or; maybe; perhaps

1169. 还是/hái shì/ - or; nevertheless

1170. 不仅/bù jǐn/ - not only

1171. 不但/bú dàn/ - not only

1172. 而且/ér qiě/ - but also

1173. 然而/rán ér/ - however; but; yet

1174. 可是/kě shì/ - but; however

1175. 不过/bú guò/ - but; however; only; no more than

我可以去，不过你得跟我一起。- I'll go, but you have to go with me.

他不过是一个部门经理。- He's only a department manager.

这座城市不过三十万人。- There are no more than 300,000 people in this city.

1176. 只要/zhǐ yào/ - if only; as long as

1177. 不管/bù guǎn/ - regardless of; no matter (what, when, how, which)

1178. 无论/wú lùn/ - no matter what; no matter how; regardless of

1179. 并且/bìng qiě/ - moreover; furthermore

1180. 因此/yīn cǐ/ - as a result; consequently

1181. 于是/yú shì/ - hence; as a result; consequently

1182. 否则/fǒu zé/ - if not; otherwise

1183. 即使/jí shǐ/ - even if; even though

1184. 尽管/jìn guǎn/ - despite; although; even though; do not hesitate (to ask, complain, etc.); (go ahead and do something) without hesitating

1185. 而 /ér/ - but; and; (indicates changes of state, contrast, causal relation, etc.)

Prepositions can be put before a noun or pronoun to form a prepositional phrase indicating time, place, direction, object, reason, manner, the passive, companion, exclusion, etc.

1186. 在 /zài/ - (located) at; (to be) in; (indicating an action in progress)

1187. 从 /cóng/ - from; via

1188. 比 /bǐ/ - used for comparison; to gesture (with hands); ratio
我比他高。- I'm taller than him.
她朝服务员比了一个手势。- She gestured to the waiter.
下面的图表显示了个人负债与收入之比。- The bottom chart shows the ratio of personal debt to personal income.

1189. 离 /lí/ - (in giving distances) from
这里离火车站多远？- How far from here to the train station?

1190. 为了 /wèi le/ - in order to; so as to

1191. 除了 /chú le/ - except; in addition to; apart from

1192. 被 /bèi/ - by (indicates passive-voice sentences or clauses)

1193. 关于 /guān yú/ - with regards to; about; concerning

1194. 经过 /jīng guò/ - after; to go through; to pass

1195. 往 /wǎng/ - to or towards (a direction or a place)

1196. 由于 /yóu yú/ - as a result of; owing to; due to; because

1197. 对于 /duì yú/ - with regards to; regarding

1198. 按照 /àn zhào/ - according to; in accordance with

1199. 随着 /suí zhe/ - along with

1200. 跟 /gēn/ - with; to

Section 2

LEARN 1,300 OTHER WORDS

This part will require you to have mastered a large number of words and sentence patterns. Some are more often used in oral language, and some in written forms. This part also has higher requirements in speaking, reading, listening, and writing.

Be patient and look for shortcuts by grasping the key points. Though the content in this part may be overwhelming, some words are basic and commonly used. As they are fundamentals, they will require your careful attention.

Chapter 6. Nouns (A ~ Q)

1201. 报社/bào shè/ - newspaper office

1202. 岸/àn/ - shore

1203. 爱心/ài xīn/ - compassion

1204. 傍晚/bàng wǎn/ - at dusk; nightfall

1205. 包裹/bāo guǒ/ - package; parcel; to wrap up

1206. 宝贝/bǎo bèi/ - baby; treasure

1207. 保险/bǎo xiǎn/ - insurance; to insure

1208. 报告/bào gào/ - report; to report

1209. 背景/bèi jǐng/ - background

1210. 被子/bèi zi/ - quilt

1211. 本科/běn kē/ - undergraduate course; undergraduate

1212. 本领/běn lǐng/ - skill; ability; capability

他的本领就是这么得来的。- This is how he acquired his skill.

1213. 本质/běn zhì/ - nature; essence

有人可能认为抽烟从本质上说就具有成瘾性。- One could argue that smoking, by its very nature, is addictive.

1214. 比例/bǐ lì/ - proportion

1215. 鞭炮/biān pào/ - firecracker

1216. 标点/biāo diǎn/ - punctuation

1217. 标志/biāo zhì / - sign; mark; symbol; to indicate; to mark
这标志着人类历史新纪元的开始。- It marks the beginning of a new era in human history.

1218. 表面/biǎo miàn/ - surface

1219. 表情/biǎo qíng/ - expression

1220. 冰激凌/bīng jī líng/ - ice cream

1221. 病毒/bìng dú/ - virus

1222. 玻璃/bō li/ - glass

1223. 博物馆/bó wù guǎn/ - museum

1224. 脖子/bó zi/ - neck

1225. 布/bù/ - cloth

1226. 部门/bù mén/ - department

1227. 步骤/bù zhòu/ - step

1228. 财产/cái chǎn/ - property; assets

1229. 彩虹/cǎi hóng/ - rainbow

1230. 参考/cān kǎo/ - reference; to refer

1231. 操场/cāo chǎng/ - playground

1232. 叉子/chā zi/ - folk

1233. 差距/chā jù/ - disparity

1234. 产品/chǎnpǐn/ - product; merchandise

1235. 长途/chángtú/ - long distance

1236. 常识/chángshí/ - common sense

1237. 车库/chē kù/ - garage

1238. 车厢/chē xiāng/ - carriage

1239. 程度/chéng dù/ - degree; extent

1240. 程序/chéng xù/ - procedure; computer program

1241. 成分/chéng fèn/ - composition

1242. 成果/chéng guǒ/ - achievement

1243. 成就/chéng jiù/ - accomplishment

1244. 成语/chéng yǔ/ - idiom; saying; set expression

1245. 成人/chéng réng/ – adult

1246. 池塘/chí táng/ – pond

1247. 尺子/chǐ zi/ – ruler (measuring instrument)

1248. 翅膀/chì bǎng/ – wing

1249. 充电器/chōng diàn qì/ – (battery) charger

1250. 宠物/chǒng wù/ – pet

1251. 抽屉/chōu ti/ – drawer

1252. 出口/chū kǒu/ – exit

1253. 除夕/chú xī/ – Chinese New Year's Eve

1254. 传说/chuán shuō/ – legend

1255. 传统/chuán tǒng/ – tradition; traditional

1256. 窗帘/chuāng lián/ – window curtains

1257. 词汇/cí huì/ – vocabulary

1258. 醋/cù/ – vinegar

1259. 措施/cuò shī/ – measure; step (to be taken)

1260. 大厦/dà shà/ – mansion

1261. 大象/dà xiàng/ – elephant

1262. 贷款/dài kuǎn/ – loan; to loan; to provide a loan

1263. 待遇/dài yù/ – treatment (in the company)

1264. 单位/dān wèi/ – unit (to measure); one's workplace

1265. 单元/dān yuán/ – unit (as an entity)

1266. 胆小鬼/dǎn xiǎo guǐ/ – coward

1267. 导演/dǎo yǎn/ – director (film, etc.)

1268. 岛屿/dǎo yǔ/ – island

1269. 道德/dào dé/ – morality; ethics; moral

1270. 道理/dào li/ – reason; logic

她详细说明了这件事的道理。– She explained the logic behind this issue.

1271. 滴/dī/ – a drop; to drip

1272. 敌人/dí rén/ – enemy

1273. 地理/dì lǐ/ - geography

1274. 地区/dì qū/ - area; region; regional

1275. 地毯/dì tǎn/ - carpet

1276. 地位/dì wèi/ - (social, etc.) status; position

1277. 地震/dì zhè/ - earthquake

1278. 点心/diǎn xin/ - pastry; dessert

1279. 电池/diàn chí/ - battery

1280. 电台/diàn tái/ - radio station

1281. 顶/dǐng/ - top; to carry on the head; to push from below or behind; to go against; to retort; to gore; to substitute; to replace; to hold on; measure word for hats, tents, etc.

山顶被积雪覆盖。 - The mountaintop was covered with snow.

印度人能用头顶着东西。 - Some Indians carry things on their head.

嫩芽把土顶起来了。 - The sprouts have pushed up the earth.

我们不得不顶风前进。 - We have to go against the wind.

我不想顶你。 - I don't want to retort you.

这牛老顶人。 - This bull gores people all the time.

患病工人的活儿他顶了。 - He substituted for the worker who was ill.

你必须快点来顶我。 - You must come quickly to replace me.

你还能再顶一会吗？ - Can you hold on a little longer?

1282. 洞/dòng/ - hole

1283. 动画片/dòng huà piàn/ - cartoon

1284. 豆腐/dòu fu/ - tofu; bean curd

1285. 对比/duì bǐ/ - contrast

1286. 对手/duì shǒu/ - opponent

1287. 对象/duì xiàng/ - boyfriend or girlfriend; object; target; partner

这是我对象。- This is my partner.

他成了被嘲弄和鄙视的对象。- He became the object of ridicule and scorn.

他的古怪使他成为他们取笑的对象。- His odd ideas made him the target of their jokes

她到处为儿子物色对象。- She's looking for a suitable partner for her son.

1288. 耳环/ěr huán/ - earring

1289. 发票/fā piào/ - invoice

1290. 罚款/fá kuǎn/ - penalty; fine (monetary)

1291. 法院/fǎ yuàn/ - court

1292. 方/fāng/ - Fang (surname)

1293. 方案/fāng àn/ - plan; proposal

1294. 方式/fāng shì/ - way (of life); mode

1295. 肥皂/féi zào/ - soap

1296. 废话/fèi huà/ - nonsense

1297. 风格/fēng gé/ - style

1298. 风景/fēng jǐng/ - scenery; landscape

1299. 风俗/fēng sú/ - social custom

1300. 风险/fēng xiǎn/ - risk

1301. 服装/fú zhuāng/ - clothing; clothes

1302. 妇女/fù nǚ/ - woman

1303. 盖/gài/ - lid; to build; to cover

我的杯盖哪去了？- Where is the lid of my cup?

他们在一周内盖起了一家医院。- They managed to build a hospital within a week.

下雨了; 找些东西把粮食盖一下。- It's raining; find something to cover the grain.

1304. 概念/gài niàn/ - concept

1305. 感想/gǎn xiǎng/ - thoughts; reflections

1306. 钢铁/gāng tiě/ - steel

1307. 隔壁/gé bì/ - next door

1308. 个性/gè xìng/ - personality

1309. 根/gēn/ - root; measure word for long slender objects, such as cigarettes, chopsticks, etc.

1310. 公寓/gōng yù/ - apartment; flat

1311. 公元/gōng yuán/ - (year) AD

1312. 公主/gōng zhǔ/ - princess

1313. 功能/gōng néng/ - function

1314. 工厂/gōng chǎng/ - factory

1315. 工程师/gōng chéng shī/ - engineer

1316. 工人/gōng rén/ - worker

1317. 工具/gōng jù/ - tool

1318. 工业/gōng yè/ - industry

1319. 姑姑/gū gu/ - aunt (paternal)

1320. 姑娘/gū niang/ - girl; young female

1321. 古代/gǔ dài/ - ancient times

1322. 股票/gǔ piào/ - stock (market); share

1323. 骨头/gú tou/ - bone

1324. 官/guān/ - official; officer

1325. 观点/guān diǎn/ - viewpoint; opinion

1326. 观念/guān niàn/ - general impression

1327. 管子/guǎn zi/ - tube; pipe; drinking straw

1328. 冠军/guàn jūn/ - champion

1329. 光盘/guāng pán/ - disc; to clean up the food on the plate

1330. 广场/guǎng chǎng/ - plaza; a public square

1331. 规矩/guī ju/ - rule

如果你守规矩，你就不大会遇到麻烦。- If you follow the rules, you are not likely to get into trouble.

1332. 规律/guī lǜ/ - regular pattern; law (of science, etc.)

1333. 规模/guī mó/ - scale

1334. 规则/guī zé/ - rule; regulation; prescribed procedure

有规则必有例外。- There are exceptions to the rules.

1335. 柜台/guì tái/ - (sales) counter

1336. 锅/guō/ - wok

1337. 国庆节/guó qìng jié/ - National Day

1338. 国王/guó wáng/ - king

1339. 果实/guǒ shí/ - (ripened) fruit; fruits (of one's labor)

1340. 海关/hǎi guān/ - custom

1341. 海鲜/hǎi xiān/ - seafood

1342. 行业/háng yè/ - business field

1343. 和平/hé píng/ - peace

1344. 合同/hé tong/ - contract

1345. 核心/hé xīn/ - core

1346. 后果/hòu guǒ/ - consequence

1347. 壶/hú/ - pot; measure word for bottled liquid

1348. 蝴蝶/hú dié/ - butterfly

1349. 胡同/hú tong/ - alley

1350. 胡须/hú xū/ - beard

1351. 花生/huā shēng/ - peanut

1352. 滑冰/huá bīng/ - ice skating

1353. 华裔/huá yì/ - ethnic Chinese

1354. 话题/huà tí/ - topic

1355. 化学/huà xué/ - chemistry; chemical

1356. 幻想/huàn xiǎng/ - delusion; fantasy

1357. 黄瓜/huáng guā/ - cucumber

1358. 黄金/huáng jīn/ - gold

1359. 皇帝/huáng dì/ - emperor
1360. 皇后/huáng hòu/ - empress
1361. 灰/huī/ - ash; dust; gray
1362. 灰尘/huī chén/ - dust
1363. 汇率/huì lǜ/ - exchange rate
1364. 婚礼/hūn lǐ/ - wedding
1365. 婚姻/hūn yīn/ - marriage
1366. 火柴/huǒ chái/ - match (for lighting a fire)
1367. 伙伴/huǒ bàn/ - companion
1368. 机器/jī qi/ - machine
1369. 肌肉/jī ròu/ - muscle
1370. 集体/jí tǐ/ - team; collective

这是集体的决定。- It was a collective decision.
我们是一个集体。- We are a team.

1371. 急诊/jí zhěn/ - emergency (medical) treatment
1372. 纪录/jì lù/ - record

该纪录保持了 13 年，无人能破。- This record figure was unequalled for 13 years.

1373. 纪律/jì lǜ/ - discipline
1374. 记忆/jì yì/ - memory
1375. 嘉宾/jiā bīn/ - esteemed guest; honored guest
1376. 家庭/jiā tíng/ - family
1377. 家务/jiā wù/ - household duties; housework
1378. 家乡/jiā xiāng/ - hometown
1379. 夹子/jiā zi/ - clip; clamp
1380. 假设/jiǎ shè/ - hypothesis; suppose that
1381. 嫁妆/jià zhuang/ - dowry
1382. 价值/jià zhí/ - value; worth
1383. 肩膀/jiān bǎng/ - shoulder

1384. 间距/jiān jù/ - spacing

这是间距问题导致的错误。- This mistake was due to a spacing problem.

1385. 兼职/jiān zhí/ - part time

1386. 简历/jiǎn lì/ - resume

1387. 剪刀/jiǎn dāo/ - scissors

1388. 健身房/jiàn shēn fáng/ - gym

1389. 建筑/jiàn zhù/ - building

1390. 键盘/jiàn pán/ - keyboard

1391. 讲座/jiǎng zuò/ - lecture

1392. 酱油/jiàng yóu/ - soy sauce

1393. 交际/jiāo jì/ - social intercourse.

1394. 郊区/jiāo qū/ - suburban district; outskirts

1395. 胶水/jiāo shuǐ/ - glue

1396. 角度/jiǎo dù/ - angle; point of view

1397. 教材/jiào cái/ - teaching material

1398. 教练/jiào liàn/ - coach

1399. 教训/jiào xun/ - lesson

公司没能从这次经历中吸取任何教训。- The company failed to learn any lessons from this experience.

1400. 阶段/jiē duàn/ - stage; phase

新体系仍处于规划阶段。- The new system is still in the planning stages.

1401. 结构/jié gòu/ - structure

1402. 结论/jié lùn/ - conclusion

1403. 解说员/jiě shuō yuán/ - commentator

1404. 借口/jiè kǒu/ - excuse

1405. 戒指/jiè zhi/ - (finger) ring

1406. 金属/jīn shǔ/ - metal

1407. 近代/jìn dài/ - modern times

1408. 精力/jīng lì/ - vitality; stamina

1409. 景色/jǐng sè/ - scenery; scene; landscape

1410. 酒吧/jiǔ bā/ - pub

1411. 救护车/jiù hù chē/ - ambulance

1412. 舅舅/jiù jiu/ - uncle (mother's brother)

1413. 桔子/jú zǐ/ - tangerine

1414. 聚会/jù huì/ - party; gathering; to get together

1415. 俱乐部/jù lè bù/ - club

1416. 决赛/jué sài/ - finals (of a competition)

1417. 决心/jué xīn/ - determination; to make up one's mind

1418. 角色/jiǎo sè/ - role; character in a novel, play, movie, etc.

1419. 军事/jūn shì/ - military

1420. 卡车/kǎ chē/ - truck

1421. 开幕式/kāi mù shì/ - opening ceremony

1422. 开水/kāi shuǐ/ - boiled water

1423. 烤鸭/kǎo yā/ - roast duck

1424. 课程/kè chéng/ - course

1425. 客厅/kè tīng/ - living room

1426. 空间/kōng jiān/ - space

1427. 口味/kǒu wèi/ - tastes (in food); flavor; a person's preferences

如你所见，这些年来我的口味变了。- My preferences have changed a lot over the years, as you can see.

1428. 会计/kuài jì/ - accountant

1429. 矿泉水/kuàng quán shuǐ/ - mineral water

1430. 昆虫/kūn chóng/ - insect

1431. 辣椒/là jiāo/ - hot pepper; chili

1432. 蜡烛/là zhú/ - candle

1433. 狼/láng/ - wolf

1434. 劳动/láo dòng/ - (physical) labor

1435. 老百姓/lǎo bǎi xìng/ - ordinary people

1436. 老板/lǎo bǎn/ - boss

1437. 老婆/lǎo po/ - wife

1438. 老鼠/lǎo shǔ/ - rat; mouse

1439. 姥姥/lǎo lao/ - grandmother (maternal)

1440. 雷/léi/ - thunder

1441. 类型/lèi xíng/ - type

1442. 梨/lí/ - pear

1443. 理论/lǐ lùn/ - theory

1444. 理由/lǐ yóu/ - reason

1445. 礼拜天/lǐ bài tiān/ - Sunday

1446. 力量/lì liang/ - power; strength

1447. 利润/lì rùn/ - profit

1448. 利息/lì xī/ - interest (on loans or savings)

1449. 利益/lì yì/ - benefit

1450. 连续剧/lián xù jù/ - soap opera

1451. 粮食/liáng shí/ - grain

1452. 列车/liè chē/ - train

1453. 铃/líng/ - bell

1454. 零件/líng jiàn/ - component; part

你们厂有没有这台机器的备用零件？- Does your company have any spare parts for this machine?

1455. 零钱/líng qián/ - change (of money)

1456. 零食/líng shí/ - snack

1457. 领导/lǐng dǎo/ - leader; to lead

我们需要你来领导大家。- We need you to lead us.

1458. 领域/lǐng yù/ - domain

1459. 龙/lóng/ - dragon

1460. 陆地/lù dì/ - dry land

1461. 论文/lùn wén/ - thesis

1462. 逻辑/luó ji/ - logic

1463. 麦克风/mài kè fēng/ - microphone

1464. 馒头/mán tou/ - steamed bun

1465. 毛/máo/ - hair; surname Mao

1466. 毛病/máo bing/ - wrong

你有什么毛病？- What's wrong with you?

1467. 矛盾/máo dùn/ - contradictory

1468. 贸易/mào yì/ - (commercial) trade

1469. 眉毛/méi mao/ - eyebrow

1470. 媒体/méi tǐ/ - media

1471. 煤炭/méi tàn/ - coal

1472. 美术/měi shù/ - art

1473. 魅力/mèi lì/ - charm

1474. 谜语/mí yǔ/ - riddle

1475. 蜜蜂/mì fēng/ - bee

1476. 秘密/mì mì/ - secret

1477. 秘书/mì shū/ - secretary

1478. 棉花/mián hua/ - cotton

1479. 民主/mín zhǔ/ - democracy; democratic

1480. 明信片/míng xìn piàn/ - postcard

1481. 明星/míng xīng/ - celebrity; star (of movie, etc.)

1482. 名牌/míng pái/ - famous brand

1483. 名片/míng piàn/ - name card

1484. 名胜古迹/míng sheng gǔ jì/ - historical sites and scenic spots

1485. 命运/mìng yùn/ - destiny; fate

1486. 摩托车/mó tuō chē/ - motorcycle

1487. 目标/mù biāo/ - target; goal

1488. 目录/mù lù/ - catalog; table of contents

1489. 木头/mù tou/ - wood; blockhead

他简直是个木头，根本不懂得如何表达情感。- He's a blockhead with no idea how to express his feelings.

1490. 脑袋/nǎo dɑi/ - head

1491. 内部/nèi bù/ - inside (part, section); internal

1492. 内科/nèi kē/ - internal medicine

1493. 能源/néng yuán/ - power source

1494. 年代/nián dài/ - era; a decade of a century

1495. 搞年纪/nián jì/ - age

1496. 牛仔裤/niú zī kù/ - jeans

1497. 农民/nóng mín/ - farmer

1498. 农业/nóng yè/ - agriculture

1499. 女士/nǚ shì/ - madam

1500. 排球/pái qiú/ - volleyball

1501. 派/pài/ - pie; to send; to assign

他被派到这儿监视我。- He's been sent here to keep an eye on me.

不久，老板派他到一个新的工作岗位。- Soon, the boss assigned him to a new post.

1502. 盆/pén/ - basin

1503. 拼音/pīn yīn/ - Pinyin

1504. 频道/pín dào/ - channel

1505. 品种/pǐn zhǒng/ - breed

1506. 平衡/píng héng/ - balance

1507. 期间/qī jiān/ - period

1508. 奇迹/qí jì/ - miracle; miraculous

1509. 企业/qǐ yè/ - enterprise

1510. 气氛/qì fēn/ - atmosphere

1511. 汽油/qì yóu/ - gasoline

1512. 前途/qián tú/ - outlook (of the future); vision

1513. 枪/qiāng/ – gun

1514. 墙/qiáng/ – wall

1515. 青春/qīng chūn/ – youth

1516. 青少年/qīng shào nián/ – youngster

1517. 情景/qíng jǐng/ – scene

1518. 情绪/qíng xù/ – feeling

1519. 趋势/qū shì/ – trend

1520. 权力/quán lì/ – authority; power

在民主政体中，权力必须分制。– In a democracy, power must be divided.

只有经理才有权力签支票。– Only the manager has the authority to sign checks.

1521. 权利/quán lì/ – privilege; right

在我国女性享有同男性一样的权利。– Women in our country enjoy equal rights with men.

他显然滥用了这项权利。– He's obviously abusing the privilege.

Chapter 7 Nouns (R ~ Z)

1522. 人才/rén cái/ - talented person

1523. 人口/rén kǒu/ - population

1524. 人类/rén lèi/ - humanity; human race; mankind

1525. 人生/rén shēng/ - (human) life

1526. 人事/rén shì/ - human resources

1527. 人物/rén wù/ - character (in a movie or book)

1528. 人员/rén yuán/ - personnel

1529. 日程/rì chéng/ - schedule; itinerary

1530. 日历/rì lì/ - calendar

1531. 日期/rì qī/ - date

1532. 日用品/rì yòng pǐn/ - everyday items

1533. 荣誉/róng yù/ - honor

她用荣誉换取财富。- She exchanged honor for wealth.

1534. 嗓子/sǎng zi/ - throat; voice

我嗓子疼。- I have a sore throat.

她有副嗓子。- She has a beautiful voice.

1535. 沙漠/shā mò/ - desert

1536. 沙滩/shā tān/ - beach

1537. 闪电/shǎn diàn/ - lightning

1538. 扇子/shàn zi/ - fan

我们的扇子分三大类：纸扇，绸扇和檀香木扇。- We have three major types of fan: paper, silk, and sandalwood.

1539. 商品/shāng pǐn/ - commodity; merchandise

1540. 商业/shāng yè/ - commerce

1541. 勺子/sháo zi/ - spoon; ladle; scoop

1542. 蛇/shé/ - snake

1543. 舌头/shé tou/ - tongue

1544. 设备/shè bèi/ - equipment; facility

增加了生产设备后，我们要做广告争取更多客户。- Having increased our manufacturing capabilities, we've begun advertising to obtain more clients.

他们公司提供厨房设备。- Their company supplies kitchen equipment.

1545. 设施/shè shī/ - facility; installation

我们城市需要更多的娱乐设施。- Our city needs more amusement facilities.

该建筑被改造成了一处秘密军事设施。- The building was turned into a secret military installation.

1546. 摄影/shè yǐng/ - photography

1547. 身材/shēn cái/ - build (height and weight)

1548. 身份/shēn fèn/ - identity; dignity

他并不认为这么做有失身份。- He did not consider it's beneath his dignity to do these things.

1549. 神话/shén huà/ - fairy tale

1550. 神经/shén jīng/ - nerve

1551. 声调/shēng diào/ - tone

1552. 绳子/shéng zi/ - rope

1553. 胜利/shèng lì/ - victory

1554. 诗/shī/ - poem

1555. 失眠/shī mián/ - insomnia

1556. 时代 /shí dài/ – era

1557. 时刻 /shí kè/ – moment; always

正是这些开心的时刻让生活有了意义。– Those are the happy moments which make life worth living.

敌人时刻都在谋划着。– The enemy is always scheming and plotting.

1558. 时期 /shí qī/ – a period in time or history

1559. 实话 /shí huà/ – truth

快说实话！– Tell the truth!

1560. 实习 /shí xí/ – internship

1561. 食物 /shí wù/ – food

1562. 石头 /shí tou/ – stone

1563. 试卷 /shì juàn/ – test paper

1564. 士兵 /shì bīng/ – soldier

1565. 事实 /shì shí/ – fact

1566. 事物 /shì wù/ – thing

他们可以参观许多地方并且看到许多事物。– They can visit many places and see many things.

1567. 收获 /shōu huò/ – harvest

1568. 收据 /shōu jù/ – receipt

1569. 手术 /shǒu shù/ – surgery

1570. 手套 /shǒu tào/ – glove; mitten

1571. 手续 /shǒu xù/ – formality

1572. 手指 /shǒu zhǐ/ – finger

1573. 寿命 /shòu mìng/ – life expectancy

1574. 书架 /shū jià/ – bookshelf

1575. 蔬菜 /shū cài/ – vegetable

1576. 梳子 /shū zi/ – comb

1577. 鼠标 /shǔ biāo/ – mouse (computing)

1578. 数据 /shù jù/ – data

1579. 税/shuì/ - tax

1580. 丝绸/sī chóu/ - silk

1581. 思想/sī xiǎng/ - thinking

1582. 寺庙/sì miào/ - temple

1583. 宿舍/sù shè/ - dormitory

1584. 损失/sǔn shī/ - loss; to lose

1585. 塔/tǎ/ - tower

1586. 台阶/tái jiē/ - step (over obstacle)

1587. 太极拳/tài jí quán/ - Tai Chi

1588. 太太/tài tai/ - Mrs.

1589. 桃/táo/ - peach

1590. 特征/tè zhēng/ - distinctive feather

1591. 提纲/tí gāng/ - outline

1592. 题目/tí mù/ - subject; topic

我对这个题目没兴趣。- I'm not interested in this subject.

他买了许多与此题目有关的书。- He bought many books relating to this topic.

1593. 体积/tǐ jī/ - volume

1594. 天空/tiān kōng/ - sky

1595. 田野/tián yě/ - field

这是一种田野里常见的花。- It's a flower common in the field.

1596. 通讯/tōng xùn/ - communication

他们的通讯系统效率低下。- Their communications systems are extremely inefficient.

1597. 铜/tóng/ - copper

1598. 土地/tǔ dì/ - land

1599. 土豆/tǔ dòu/ - potato

1600. 兔子/tù zǐ/ - rabbit

1601. 优势/yōu shì/ - advantage; superiority

1602. 外公/wài gōng/ - grandfather (maternal)

1603. 外交/wài jiāo/ - diplomacy; diplomatic
1604. 玩具/wán jù/ - toy
1605. 王子/wáng zǐ/ - prince
1606. 网络/wǎng luò/ - network
1607. 微笑/wēi xiào/ - smile
1608. 围巾/wéi jīn/ - scarf
1609. 尾巴/wěi ba/ - tail
1610. 胃/wèi/ - stomach
1611. 胃口/wèi kǒu/ - appetite
1612. 位置/wèi zhi/ - location
1613. 未来/wèi lái/ - future
1614. 卫生间/wèi shēng jiān/ - bathroom; toilet
1615. 文件/wén jiàn/ - document; file
1616. 文具/wén jù/ - stationery
1617. 文学/wén xué/ - literature
1618. 吻/wěn/ - kiss; to kiss
1619. 卧室/wò shì/ - bedroom
1620. 屋子/wū zi/ - house
1621. 武器/wǔ qì/ - weapon
1622. 武术/wǔ shù/ - martial art
1623. 雾/wù/ - fog; mist
1624. 物理/wù lǐ/ - physics; physical
1625. 物质/wù zhì/ - matter; substance
他专门研究暗物质。 - He specializes in dark matter.
1626. 系统/xì tǒng/ - system
1627. 细节/xì jié/ - detail
1628. 戏剧/xì jù/ - drama
1629. 夏令营/xià lìng yíng/ - summer camp
1630. 县/xiàn/ - county
1631. 现金/xiàn jīn/ - cash

1632. 现象 /xiàn xiàng/ - phenomenon
1633. 香肠 /xiāng cháng/ - sausage
1634. 项链 /xiàng liàn/ - necklace
1635. 项目 /xiàng mù/ - project
1636. 橡皮 /xiàng pí/ - eraser
1637. 象棋 /xiàng qí/ - Chinese Chess
1638. 小吃 /xiǎo chī/ - snack
1639. 小伙子 /xiǎo huǒ zi/ - young man
1640. 小麦 /xiǎo mài/ - wheat
1641. 小偷 /xiǎo tōu/ - thief
1642. 效率 /xiào lǜ/ - efficiency
1643. 心理 /xīn lǐ/ - mental; psychological
1644. 心脏 /xīn zàng/ - heart
1645. 信封 /xìn fēng/ - envelop
1646. 信号 /xìn hào/ - signal
1647. 信息 /xìn xī/ - information; news; message
1648 行动 /xíng dòng/ - action; to more
1649. 行人 /xíng rén/ - pedestrian
1650. 行为 /xíng wéi/ - behavior
1651. 形式 /xíng shì/ - form

我反对任何形式地狩猎。- I am against hunting in any form.

1652. 形势 /xíng shì/ - situation

他非常周密地分析了形势。- He analyzed the situation very deeply.

1653. 形状 /xíng zhuàng/ - shape
1654. 性质 /xìng zhì/ - nature

他对自己使命的确切性质还不清楚。- He was not clear on the precise nature of his mission.

1655. 胸 /xiōng/ - chest
1656. 兄弟 /xiōng di/ - dude

1657. 休闲/xiū xián/ - leisure

1658. 学历/xué lì/ - educational background

1659. 学期/xué qī/ - semester

1660. 学术/xué shù/ - academic

1661. 血/xiě/ - blood

1662. 演讲/yǎn jiǎng/ - lecture

1663. 宴会/yàn huì/ - banquet

1664. 阳台/yáng tái/ - balcony; porch

1665. 样式/yàng shì/ - style

1666. 腰/yāo/ - waist

1667. 夜/yè/ - night

冬天昼短夜长。- In winter the days are short and the nights long.

1668. 液体/yè tǐ/ - liquid

1669. 业务/yè wù/ - business; vocational work

我有一家药店，想要扩大业务。- I owned a drugstore and wanted to expand the business.

管理咨询是我公司的一项核心业务。- Management consulting is a major vocation in the company.

1670. 一辈子/yí bèi zi/ - for a lifetime

1671. 疑问/yí wèn/ - question; doubt

1672. 意见/yì jian/ - opinion; suggestion

1673. 意外/yì wài/ - accident; unforeseen

他死于一场意外。- He died in an accident.

这是她好运中的一次意外挫折。- It was an unforeseen setback in her fortunes.

1674. 意义/yì yi/ - meaning

1675. 义务/yì wù/ - obligation

1676. 因素/yīn sù/ - factor

1677. 银/yín/ - silver

1678. 英雄/yīng xióng/ - hero
1679. 营养/yíng yǎng/ - nutrition; nourishment
1680. 影子/yǐng zi/ - shadow
1681. 硬币/yìng bì/ - coin
1682. 硬件/yìng jiàn/ - hardware
1683. 勇气/yǒng qì/ - courage
1684. 用途/yòng tú/ - purpose
他坚称这笔捐款将用于国际用途。- He has maintained that the money was donated for international purposes.
1685. 邮局/yóu jú/ - post office
1686. 幼儿园/yòu ér yuán/ - kindergarten
1687. 语气/yǔ qì/ - tone (of speech)
医生的语气很严肃。- The doctor's tone was serious.
1688. 宇宙/yǔ zhòu/ - universe
1689. 预报/yù bào/ - forecast; to forecast
1690. 玉米/yù mǐ/ - corn
1691. 元旦/yuán dàn/ - New Year's Day
1692. 缘故/yuán gù/ - reason
1693. 原料/yuán liào/ - raw material
1694. 原则/yuán zé/ - in principle
1695. 员工/yuán gōng/ - employee
1696. 愿望/yuàn wàng/ - wish
1697. 乐器/yuè qì/ - musical instrument
1698. 运气/yùn qi/ - luck
1699. 灾害/zāi hài/ - disaster
1700. 战争/zhàn zhēng/ - war
1701. 长辈/zhǎng bèi/ - one's elders
1702. 账户/zhàng hù/ - account
1703. 哲学/zhé xué/ - philosophy

1704. 真理/zhēn lǐ/ - truth

真理面前，人人平等。- Everyone is equal before the truth.

1705. 枕头/zhěn tou/ - pillow

1706. 整体/zhěng tǐ/ - whole

城市规划将城市视为一个有机的整体。- Urban planning treats the city as an organic whole.

1707. 政府/zhèng fǔ/ - government

1708. 政治/zhèng zhì/ - politics; political

1709. 证件/zhèng jiàn/ - credentials

1710. 证据/zhèng jù/ - evidence; proof

1711. 支票/zhī piào/ - check

1712. 执照/zhí zhào/ - license

1713. 制度/zhì dù/ - (political, administrative, etc.) system

1714. 智慧/zhì huì/ - wisdom

1715. 秩序/zhì xù/ - order

旧的社会秩序一去不复返。- The old social order was gone forever.

警察是法律和秩序地守护者。- The police are guardians of law and order.

1716. 志愿者/zhì yuàn zhě/ - volunteer

1717. 钟/zhōng/ - clock; Zhong (surname)

1718. 中介/zhōng jiè/ - agency; mediation

我们得通过中介雇佣保姆。- We had to hire a nanny through an agency.

该应用提供了位置、协议和一系列中介功能。- The application provides location, protocol, and a number of mediation capabilities.

1719. 中心/zhōng xīn/ - center

1720. 中旬/zhōng xún/ - middle of a month

1721. 种类/zhǒng lèi/ - type

1722. 重量/zhòng liàng/ - weight

1723. 竹子/zhú zǐ/ - bamboo

1724. 主人/zhǔ rén/ - host; hostess; master

旧社会的奴隶变成了新社会的主人。- The slaves of the old society have become the masters of the new society.

1725. 主任/zhǔ rèng/ - director; head (of an office, etc.)

1726. 主题/zhǔ tí/ - theme

1727. 主席/zhǔ xí/ - chairperson

1728. 主张/zhǔ zhāng/ - proposal; advocacy; to stand for

两种主张都有道理。- Both proposals sound reasonable.

我支持你自由贸易的主张。- I support your advocacy of free trade.

他主张将国家从教条的控制下解放出来。- He stands for freeing the country from the grip of dogma.

1729. 专家/zhuān jiā/ - expert

1730. 资格/zī ge/ - qualification

1731. 资金/zī jīn/ - funds; funding

1732. 资源/zī yuán/ - resource

1733. 姿势/zī shì/ - posture

1734. 字母/zì mǔ/ - letter (of the alphabet)

1735. 字幕/zì mù/ - subtitle

1736. 自信/zì xìn/ - self-confidence

1737. 自由/zì yóu/ - freedom; liberty

1738. 宗教/zōng jiào/ - religion

1739. 总裁/zǒng cái/ - CEO

1740. 总理/zǒng lǐ/ - premier; prime minister

1741. 总统/zǒng tǒng/ - president (of a country)

1742. 祖国/zǔ guó/ - homeland

1743. 祖先/zǔ xiān/ - ancestor

1744. 罪犯/zuì fàn/ - criminals

1745. 作品/zuò pǐn/ – work (of art, literature, etc.)
1746. 作文/zuò wén/ – composition (student essay)

Chapter 8. Verbs (A ~ L)

1747. 爱护/ài hù/ - to take care of; to cherish; to love and to protect

1748. 爱惜/ài xī/ - to cherish; to use sparingly

1749. 安慰/ān wèi/ - to comfort

1750. 安装/ān zhuāng/ - to install

1751. 熬夜/áo yè/ - to stay up late

1752. 把握/bǎ wò/ - to grasp; to seize; sure (of the outcome)

你一定要把握住这次机会。- You really need to grasp this opportunity.

我可没有把握做这件事。- I'm not sure about doing this.

1753. 摆/bǎi/ - to arrange; to put

1754. 办理/bàn lǐ/ - to handle; to deal with; to conduct

1755. 包含/bāo hán/ - to contain; to include

1756. 保持/bǎo chí/ - to keep; to maintain; to hold

几年来，我和她一直保持联系。- I kept in touch with her for several years.

该部门与化工行业保持着众多密切的联系。- The department maintains many close contacts with the chemical industry.

这样的好天气能保持多久？- How long will the fine weather hold?

1757. 保存/bǎo cún/ - to preserve; to keep; to save (computing)

这些书保存得很好。- These books are well preserved.

校长把我校的所有报告都存档保存。- The principal keeps all our school reports on file.

从扫描仪导入扫描后的图像，并保存为 JPG 文件。- Import your images from the scanner and save them as JPG files.

1758. 保留/bǎo liú/ - to retain; to preserve; to reserve

他还保留着战争年代的革命朝气。- He still retains the revolutionary fervor of the war years.

她保留了改变主意的权利。- She reserved the right to change her mind.

市政府花了不少钱来保留那座古堡。- The city government spent a lot of money to preserve the old castle.

1759. 报到/bào dào/ - to report for duty; to check in

1760. 抱怨/bào yuàn/ - to complain; complaint

1761. 背/bēi/ - to give a piggyback

/bèi/ - to recite; the back of a body or object; to turn one's back

1762. 避免/bì miǎn/ - to avoid

1763. 编辑/biān ji/ - to edit; editor

1764. 辩论/biàn lùn/ - to argue over; debate

1765. 表明/biǎo míng/ - to make clear; to indicate

我们今天的投票表明了政策得一种变化。- Our vote today indicates a change in policy.

1766. 表现/biǎo xiàn/ - to show; behavior (at school); performance (at work)

他在逆境中表现出了勇气。- He showed courage in adversity.

她因在校表现好而获奖。- She won a prize for good behavior at school.

1767. 播放/bō fàng/ - to broadcast

1768. 补充/bǔ chōng/ - to replenish; supplementary

1769. 踩/cǎi/ - to step on

1770. 采访/cǎi fǎng/ - to interview

1771. 采取/cǎi qǔ/ - to adopt or carry out (measures, policies, course of action)

1772. 参与/cān yù/ - to participate

1773. 操心/cāo xīn/ - to worry about

1774. 测验/cè yàn/ - to test; test

1775. 产生/chǎn shēng/ - to come into being; to emerge

第一个工人联盟就这样产生了。- Thus, the first worker's league came into being.

你们的会谈产生了什么结果？- What was the result of your discussion?

1776. 炒/chǎo/ - to stir-fry; to fire

他被炒了。- He was fired.

1777. 吵架/chǎo jià/ - to quarrel

1778. 趁/chèn/ - to take (advantage of); (while)

我想趁这个机会讲几句话。- I'd like to take this opportunity to say a few words.

这面得趁热吃。- Eat the noodles while they are still hot.

1779. 称/chēng/ - to weigh; to name

我们都称他铁牛。- We all call him iron ox.

1780. 称呼/chēng hu/ - to name; appellation

他被称呼为先驱。- He was called a pioneer.

他赢得了"反叛牧师"的称呼。- He earned the appellation "rebel priest".

1781. 称赞/chēng zàn/ - to praise; to compliment

1782. 承担/chéng dān/ - to undertake: to assume (responsibility, etc.)

1783. 承认/chéng rèn/ - to admit

1784. 承受/chéng shòu/ - to bear

1785. 成立/chéng lì/ - to establish; to set up

1786. 成长/chéng zhǎng/ - to grow; growth

1787. 吃亏/chī kuī/ - to be at a disadvantage; to lose out; to suffer losses

跟他做生意你是要吃亏的。- You'll suffer losses if you do business with him.

在新一轮的薪资弹性化政策中吃亏的是女性。- Women have lost out in this new pay flexibility scheme.

1788. 充满/chōng mǎn/ - to be full of; to be brimming with; to be filled with

他充满了悔恨。- He was filled with remorse.

这本书里充满了真实有趣的人物形象。- This book is full of believable interesting characters.

她两眼充满泪水。- Her eyes were brimming with tears.

1789. 重复/chóng fù/ - to repeat; to duplicate

1790. 出版/chū bǎn/ - to publish

1791. 出示/chū shì/ - to (take out and) show

请出示护照。- Please show me your passport.

1792. 出席/chū xí/ - to attend

1793. 处理/chǔ lǐ/ - to process

1794. 传播/chuán bō/ - to spread; to propagate

1795. 传染/chuán rǎn/ - to infect; contagious

1796. 闯/chuǎng/ - to break through; to temper oneself (through battling hardships)

1797. 创造/chuàng zào/ - to create; to innovate

1798. 吹/chuī/ - to blow; to bring; to play (a wind instrument); to puff; to brag; to fall through

那个男孩在吹泡泡。- The boy over there was blowing bubbles.

什么风把你吹来了？- What brings you here?

她长笛吹得不错。- She plays the flute quite well.

先别吹; 做出具体成绩来再说。- Don't brag about what you're going to do; get something done first.

他们把他吹上了天。- They talked him up (to the skies).

原来的计划吹了。- The original plan has fallen through.

1799. 辞职/cí zhí/ - to resign

1800. 刺激/cì jī/ - to stimulate; to provoke; to irritate

1801. 从事/cóng shì/ - to engage in; to undertake

1802. 促进/cù jìn/ - to promote; to boost

体育活动促进身体健康。- Physical activity promotes good health.

出口产业将促进经济发展。- The export sector will boost the economy.

1803. 促使/cù shǐ/ - to impel; to drive (someone to do something)

生产的发展促使我们不断钻研技术。- The development of production impels us continuously to study new techniques.

那么是什么促使他这么做的呢？- What drove him to do something like this?

1804. 催/cuī/ - to rush someone

1805. 存在/cún zài/ - to exist

1806. 答应/dā ying/ - to agree

1807. 达到/dá dào/ - to achieve; to attain

1808. 打工/dǎ gōng/ - to work

1809. 打交道/dǎ jiāo dào/ - to have dealings with; to deal with

不要和那个人打交道。- Don't have any dealings with that fellow.

我们经常跟他打交道。- We often deal with him.

1810. 打喷嚏/dǎ pēn tì/ - to sneeze

1811. 打听/dǎ ting/ - to ask about; to inquire about
我想跟你打听个事。- I'd like to ask you about something.
他到医院去打听她的情况。- He went to the hospital to inquire about her.

1812. 呆/dāi/ - to stay; stupid
医生劝我在家呆几天。- The doctor advised me to stay in for a few days.
他是个呆子。- He's a stupid guy.

1813. 担任/dān rèn/ - to serve as; to hold a post

1814. 耽误/dān wu/ - to delay; to waste time; to interfere with

1815. 当心/dāng xīn/ - to look out

1816. 挡/dǎng/ - to block; to hold; to stand in the way; gear
一条大河挡住了前路。- A big river blocks the way.
叫那个男孩别挡道。- Tell the boy not to stand in the way.
在山上，他得挂低速挡。- On hills, he must use low gears.
我们的军队快挡不住敌人了。- Our army can't hold back the enemy.

1817. 倒霉/dǎo méi/ - to have bad luck

1818. 导致/dǎo zhì/ - to lead to; to cause

1819. 到达/dào dá/ - to arrive

1820. 登记/dēng jì/ - to register

1821. 等待/děng dài/ - to wait for

1822. 等于/děng yú/ - to equal to

1823. 递/dì/ - to hand over; to pass on something; progressively
该委员会从政府处获得的津贴年年递减。- The grants the council received from the government was progressively reduced every year.

1824. 钓/diào/ - to fish

1825. 冻/dòng/ - to freeze

1826. 逗/dòu/ - to tease

1827. 度过/dù guò/ - to spend (time); to get through; to survive

我相信你能度过难关。- I believe you can survive this.

1828. 堆/duī/ - to pile up; pile (of things)

1829. 兑换/duì huàn/ - to convert; to exchange

1830. 对待/duì dài/ - to treat; treatment

1831. 蹲/dūn/ - to crouch

1832. 顿/dùn/ - to pause; pause; measure word for meals, beating, telling off, etc.

在讲这件事时，她顿了好几下。- While talking about it, she paused several times.

他顿了一顿，又接着说下去。- After a short pause, he went on.

1833. 躲藏/duǒ cáng/ - to hide

1834. 发表/fā biǎo/ - to publish; to issue (a statement)

我把他的草稿重新改写，并以我的名义发表了。- I rewrote his draft and published it under my name.

他发表了一个简短隐晦的声明，否认对其间谍行为的指控。- He has issued a short, cryptic statement denying the espionage charges.

1835. 发愁/fā chóu/ - to be anxious; to worry; to become sad

1836. 发抖/fā dǒu/ - to tremble

1837. 发挥/fā huī/ - to bring into play

发挥中央和地方两个积极性。- Both central and local initiatives should be brought into play.

1838. 发明/fā míng/ - to invent; invention

1839. 发言/fā yán/ - to make a speech; statement

1840. 翻/fān/ - to turn over; to flip over

1841. 反应/fǎn yìng/ - to react; reaction

1842. 妨碍/fáng ài/ - to hinder; to obstruct

1843. 分别/fēn bié/ - to part; to distinguish; difference; separately

他们已分别多年了。- They were parted for years.

你必须学会分别善恶。- You must learn to distinguish good from evil.

两者之间没有任何分别。- There is no difference between the two.

我需要分别和他们谈谈。- I need to talk with them separately.

1844. 分布/fēn bù/ - to distribute

1845. 分配/fēn pèi/ - to allocate; to assign

1846. 分手/fēn shǒu/ - to break up

1847. 分析/fēn xī/ - to analyze; analysis

1848. 奋斗/fèn dòu/ - to strive

1849. 讽刺/fěng cì/ - to satirize; sarcasm; irony

1850. 否定/fǒu dìng/ - to negate; negative (answer)

1851. 否认/fǒu rèn/ - to deny

1852. 扶/fú/ - to support with hand

1853. 辅导/fǔ dǎo/ - to coach; to give advice (in study)

1854. 复制/fù zhì/ - to copy; to duplicate

1855. 改革/gǎi gé/ - to reform; reform

1856. 改进/gǎi jìn/ - to improve; improvement

教师们如何才能改进教学以激发创造性呢？- How can faculty improve their teaching to encourage creativity?

还有改进的余地。- There is still room for improvement.

1857. 改善/gǎi shàn/ - to improve; to make better

必须兼顾发展生产和改善生活。- Consideration must be given to both the development of production and the improvement of livelihoods.

两国关系已有所改善。- The relations between the two countries have shown some improvement.

1858. 改正/gǎi zhèng/ - to correct; correction

1859. 概括/gài kuò/ - to summarize; to generalize

1860. 感激/gǎn jī/ - to express thanks; grateful

1861. 感受/gǎn shòu/ - to sense; to feel; perception

1862. 赶紧/gǎn jǐn/ - to hurry up; hurriedly

1863. 干活儿/gàn huór/ - to get to work

1864. 搞/gǎo/ - to do; to carry on; to be engaged in; to work out; to produce; to play (tricks, plots, etc.); to set up; to make (food, money, etc.); to get hold of

你脸上怎么搞的？ - What have you done to your face?

中国一直在搞计划生育。 - China has carried out birth control for quite a long time.

她丈夫是搞科学研究的。 - Her husband is engaged in scientific research.

图纸搞出来了吗？ - Has the drawing been worked out?

我们也可以搞一些这样的产品。 - We can also produce something like this.

别跟我搞花样！ - Don't play tricks on me!

当地政府打算在这里搞一个工业园。 - The local government is thinking of setting up an industrial zone here.

这些人只想搞钱。 - These people are just interested in making money.

我搞到两张音乐会的票。 - I've got hold of two tickets for the concert.

1865. 告别/gào bié/ - to say goodbye

1866. 公布/gōng bù/ - to announce

政府已经公布了一系列帮助电影业的措施。 - The government has announced a package of measures to help the film industry.

1867. 贡献/gòng xiàn/ - to contribute; contribution

1868. 沟通/gōu tōng/ - to communicate; communication

1869. 构成/gòu chéng/ - to constitute; to compose

1870. 鼓舞/gǔ wǔ/ – to boost (morale)

1871. 挂号/guà hào/ – to register (at a hospital)

1872. 拐弯/guǎi wān/ – to turn a corner

1873. 关闭/guān bì/ – to close; to shut

1874. 观察/guān chá/ – to observe; observation

1875. 光临/guāng lín/ – (it is an honor to) have you here

1876. 归纳/guī nà/ – to sum up; to conclude

1877. 滚/gǔn/ – to roll; to get lost (imperative)

1878. 过敏/guò mǐn/ – to be allergic; allergy

1879. 过期/guò qī/ – to expire; expiration

1880. 哈/hā/ – to blow one's breath; ha (laughter); aha

他在窗户玻璃上哈了一口气。 – He blew a breath of air on a windowpane.

1881. 喊/hǎn/ – to shout; to yell

1882. 合谋/hé móu/ – to plan something together

1883. 合影/hé yǐng/ – to have a group photo taken

1884. 合作/hé zuò/ – to cooperate; to collaborate; cooperation

1885. 恨/hèn/ – to hate; to regret; hate

她恨你就因为你说的那句话。 – She hates you for saying that.

我恨自己结婚太早。 – I regret that I got married so young.

爱与恨可以共存吗？ – Can love and hate coexist?

1886. 忽视/hū shì/ – to neglect; to ignore

1887. 呼吸/hū xī/ – to breathe

1888. 胡说/hú shuō/ – to talk nonsense

1889. 糊涂/hú tu/ – to be confused; muddled

1890. 划船/huá chuán/ – to paddle a boat

1891. 滑/huá/ – to slip; to slide; slippery

1892. 怀念/huái niàn/ – to cherish the memory of

1893. 缓解/huǎn jiě/ – to ease; to help relieve

1894. 挥/huī/ – to wave

1895. 挥别/huī bié/ - to wave goodbye

1896. 灰心/huī xīn/ - to be discouraged; to lose heart
别灰心！- Don't be discouraged! (Don't lose heart!)

1897. 恢复/huī fù/ - to resume; to recover; to regain; to restore
预期很快能恢复交通。- Traffic is expected to resume shortly.
我恢复了健康，并娶了那所医院一位护理我的护士。- I recovered and married one of my nurses from the hospital.
我拼命恢复自己的一点儿尊严。- I struggled to regain some dignity.
这座城市终于恢复了平静。- Peace was finally restored to the city.

1898. 回收/huí shōu/ - to recycle

1899. 回首/huí shǒu/ - to look back (on the past)

1900. 及格/jí gé/ - to pass a test

1901. 集中/jí zhōng/ - to concentrate; to focus; concentration
工业区集中在东部和西部。- The industrial districts are concentrated in the east and the west.
现在投票更趋集中了。- Voting is now more focused.
我们注意力不够集中，结果丢了球，输了比赛。- We lacked concentration, and it cost us the goal and the game.

1902. 系领带/jì lǐng dài/ - to tie one's necktie

1903. 记录/jì lù/ - to take notes; record
他的发言我都记录下来了。- I've taken notes on what he said.
对他的指控包括诈骗、行贿和伪造商业记录。- The charges against him include fraud, bribery, and falsifying business records.

1905. 纪念/jì niàn/ - to commemorate; to remember; commemorative
政府要为纪念战争死难者的举行教堂礼拜仪式。- The government is going to provide a church service to remember those who died in the war.

1906. 计算/jì suàn/ - to calculate

1907. 假装/jiǎ zhuāng/ – to pretend

1908. 嫁/jià/ – (of a woman) to marry; to marry (off a daughter)

1909. 嫁祸/jià huò/ – to shift the blame onto someone else; to frame

1910. 驾驶/jià shǐ/ – to drive (a vehicle); to pilot (a ship, a plane, etc.)

1911. 煎/jiān/ – to fry

1912. 捡/jiǎn/ – to pick up (from the ground)

1913. 健身/jiàn shēn/ – to exercise; to keep fit; to work out

1914. 建立/jiàn lì/ – to establish; to found

1915. 建设/jiàn shè/ – to construct

1916. 讲究/jiǎng jiu/ – to be fastidious about; to pay attention to
她非常讲究仪表。– She was fastidious about her appearance.
他不怎么讲究吃喝。– He doesn't pay attention to what he eats or drinks.

1917. 浇/jiāo/ – to water; to cast (molten metal); to pour liquid

1918. 交换/jiāo huàn/ – to exchange; to switch

1919. 交往/jiāo wǎng/ – to associate; to go out with; to date

1920. 接触/jiē chù/ – to contact; to touch; in touch with

1921. 接待/jiē dài/ – to receive (a visitor or a guest)

1922. 接近/jiē jìn/ – to approach someone; close to; near

1923. 接吻/jiē wěn/ – to kiss each other on the lips

1924. 接着/jiē zhe/ – to catch and hold on; to go on to do something; then; after that

1925. 节省/jié shěng/ – to save (resources, money, etc.); to cut down on

1926. 结合/jié hé/ – to combine

1927. 结算/jié suàn/ – to settle accounts; to balance accounts

1928. 结账/jié zhàng/ – to pay the bill

1929. 解放/jiě fàng/ – to emancipate; to liberate

1930. 戒/jiè/ – to give up or stop doing something

1931. 戒烟/jiè yān/ – to quit smoking

1932. 进步/jìn bù/ – to progress

1933. 进口/jìn kǒu/ – to import; imported; inlet

1934. 尽力/jìn lì/ – to spare no effort;

1935. 经商/jīng shāng/ – to be in business

1936. 经营/jīng yíng/ – to engage in (business, etc.); to operate (a store, etc.)

1937. 救/jiù/ – to rescue; to save

1938. 具备/jù bèi/ – to possess (conditions or requirements)

1939. 捐/juān/ – to donate

1940. 开发/kāi fā/ – to develop

1941. 开放/kāi fàng/ – to open to the outside world; to open (for public): to come into bloom (of flowers)

中国要进一步扩大开放范围。– China will further expand the scope of its opened-up areas.

该旅馆已向客人开放。– The hotel is now open to guests.

玫瑰花已经开放。– The roses have come into bloom.

1942. 开心/kāi xīn/ – to have a great time; to feel happy

1943. 砍/kǎn/ – to chop; to cut down

1944. 看不起/kàn bu qǐ/ – to look down upon

1945. 看望/kàn wàng/ – to pay a call to

1946. 抗议/kàng yì/ – to protest

1947. 克服/kè fú/ – to overcome

1948. 刻苦/kè kǔ/ – to study hard

他从此将会刻苦学习。– He will study harder from now on.

1949. 控制/kòng zhì/ – to control

1950. 夸张/kuā zhāng/ – to exaggerate; exaggerated

1951. 来自/lái zì/ – to come from

1952. 朗读/lǎng dú/ – to read aloud

1953. 劳驾 /láo jià/ – excuse me

1954. 离婚 /lí hūn/ – to divorce

1955. 利用 /lì yòng/ – to make use of; to take advantage of

1956. 联合 /lián hé/ – to make an alliance; to unite

1957. 恋爱 /liàn ài/ – to be in love

1958. 流传 /liú chuán/ – to spread

1959. 浏览 /liú lǎn/ – to browse; to skim over

1960. 漏 /lòu/ – to leak; to leave out (by mistake)

水从管子中漏出。– The water leaked from the pipe.

印刷工人把这一段漏了两行。– The printer has left out two lines from this paragraph.

1961. 录取 /lù qǔ/ – to enroll

1962. 录音 /lù yīn/ – to record (sound); sound recording

1963. 轮流 /lún liú/ – to take turns

1964. 落后 /luò hòu/ – to fall behind

Chapter 9 Verbs (M ~ Z)

1965. 骂/mà/ - to scold; abuse

1966. 满足/mǎn zú/ - to satisfy; to meet (the needs of); to be satisfied

为了满足好奇心，我们去了鬼屋。- To satisfy our own curiosity, we went into the haunted house.

我们可以满足你的一切需要。- We can meet all your needs.

他对自己的所得从不感到满足。- He's never satisfied with what he's got.

1967. 冒险/mào xiǎn/ - to take risks; to take chances; adventure

1968. 迷路/mí lù/ - to be lost; to lose the way

1969. 面对/miàn duì/ - to face; to confront

面对证据，他承认有罪。- Faced with the evidence, he admitted his guilt.

我们必须乐观面对未来。- We must face the future with optimism.

1970. 面临/miàn lín/ - to be confronted

她面临严峻的资金问题。- She was confronted with severe financial problems.

1971. 描写/miáo xiě/ - to describe (with writing); description (on paper)

1972. 明确/míng què/ - to clarify; to specify

1973. 命令/mìng lìng/ - to command; command

1974. 模仿/mó fǎng/ - to imitate; to mimic

1975. 念/niàn/ - to read

1976. 拍/pāi/ - to pat; to flap; to take (a photo); to clap; to shoot (a movie)

我拍了拍小狗的头。- I patted the puppy on the head.

她用报纸拍苍蝇。- She smacked the newspaper at the fly.

能和我拍张照吗？- Can you take a photo with me?

他高兴地拍起手来。- He clapped her hands in delight.

这部电影是在澳大利亚拍的。- This film was shot in Australia.

1977. 排队/pái duì/ - to line up; to form a line

1978. 盼望/pàn wàng/ - to hope for; to look forward to

1979. 赔偿/péi cháng/ - to compensate

1980. 培养/péi yǎng/ - to breed

1981. 培训/péi xù/ - to train

1982. 佩服/pèi fu/ - to admire

1983. 配合/pèi hé/ - to coordinate

1984. 碰见/pèng jiàn/ - to run into

1985. 披/pī/ - to drape over one's shoulder

1986. 批准/pī zhǔn/ - to approve

1987. 飘/piāo/ - to float in the air

1988. 漂/piāo/ - to float on the water

1989. 评价/píng jià/ - to evaluate; to assess

1990. 破产/pò chǎn/ - to go bankrupt

1991. 破坏/pò huài/ - to destroy; destruction; damage

1992. 期待/qī dài/ - to look forward to; expectation

1993. 启发/qǐ fā/ - to enlighten; to inspire

1994. 企图/qǐ tú/ - to attempt

1995. 签/qiān/ - to sign (one's name)

他即将签下一份合同。 - He's about to sign another contract.

1996. 签字/qiān zì/ - to sign (one's name); signature

在加入我们之前你需要在此签字。 - You need to sign here before joining us.

我认不出这是谁的签字。 - I cannot identify this signature.

1997. 欠/qiàn/ - to owe

1998. 强调/qiáng diào/ - to emphasize; to stress

1999. 抢/qiǎng/ - to rob

2000. 瞧/qiáo/ - to see; to look at

2001. 侵略/qīn luè/ - to invade

2002. 勤奋/qín fèn/ - to work hard; diligent

政府必须勤奋工作以重新赢得人民的信任。 - The government will have to work hard to win back the confidence of the people.

他勤奋极了。 - He is so diligent.

2003. 轻视/qīng shì/ - to despise; contempt

2004. 请求/qǐng qiú/ - to request; request

2005. 庆祝/qìng zhù/ - to celebrate

2006. 娶/qǔ/ - to marry (a woman)

2007. 取消/qǔ xiāo/ - to cancel; cancellation

2008. 去世/qù shì/ - to pass away

2009. 劝/quàn/ - to try to persuade

2010. 缺乏/quē fá/ - to lack; to be short of

2011. 确定/què dìng/ - to confirm; to be sure; to determine

你能确定吗？ - Can you confirm this?

你确定锁门了吗？ - Are you sure you locked the door?

必须进行检测以确定其对人的长期影响。 - Testing must be carried out to determine the long-term effects on humans.

2012. 确认/què rèn/ - to make an identification; to confirm; confirmation

警方正式确认了死者身份。- The police officially confirmed the identity of the deceased.

请书面确认你接受该建议。- Please confirm your acceptance of this offer in writing.

我们在等他们的书面确认。- We're waiting for written confirmation from them.

2013. 燃烧/rán shāo/ - to burn

2014. 热爱/rè ài/ - to adore

2015. 融化/róng huà/ - to melt

2016. 软件/ruǎn jiàn/ - software

2017. 洒/sǎ/ - to sprinkle; to spray

2018. 杀/shā/ - to kill

2019. 晒/shài/ - to dry in the sun; to sunbathe

2020. 删除/shān chú/ - to delete

2021. 善于/shàn yú/ - to be good at

2022. 上当/shàng dàng/ - to be fooled

2023. 舍不得/shě bu de/ - hate to part with; hate to give up or use

我舍不得你。- I hate to part from you.

看着这些菜，我都舍不得动筷子了。- These dishes are so good, I almost don't want to eat them.

2024. 设计/shè jì/ - to design; design

2025. 射击/shè jī/ - to shoot

2026. 生产/shēng chǎn/ - to manufacture; to produce; to give birth (to a child)

我的妻子即将生产。- My wife is about to give birth.

2027. 生长/shēng zhǎng/ - to grow

2028. 省略/shěng lüè/ - to omit; omission

2029. 失业/shī yè/ - to lose one's job

2030. 失去/shí qù/ - to lose

2031. 实践/shí jiàn/ - to put into practice; practices
认识从实践开始。 - Knowledge begins with practice.
下一步就是要将理论付诸实践。 - The next step is to put the theory into practice.

2032. 实现/shí xiàn/ - to come true; to realize
我的愿望实现了。 - My wishes have been realized.
他的梦想实现了。 - His dream came true.

2033. 实行/shí xíng/ - to carry out; to implement

2034. 实验/shí yàn/ - to experiment; experiment

2035. 受伤/shòu shāng/ - to be injured; to be wounded

2036. 输入/shū rù/ - to input; input

2037. 属于/shǔ yú/ - to belong to

2038. 摔倒/shuāi dǎo/ - to fall down; to throw someone to the ground

2039. 说服/shuō fú/ - to persuade; to convince

2040. 思考/sī kǎo/ - to think
显然你需要更多的时间来思考。 - It's obvious that you need more time to think.

2041. 撕/sī/ - to tear; to rip

2042. 搜索/sōu suǒ/ - to search

2043. 随手/suí shǒu/ - (to do something without extra trouble)
出门请随手关灯。 - Please switch off the lights when you leave.

2044. 缩短/suō duǎn/ - to shorten; to cut
吸烟会缩短你的寿命。 - Smoking can shorten your life.
一年的课程被缩短为六个月。 - The year-long course was cut into six months.

2045. 缩小/suō xiǎo/ - to narrow; to zoom in; to shrink

这是缩小它们之间差距的主要方法。- This is the main way we can close the distance between them.

你可以在流程上进行缩小和放大。- You can zoom in and out on the process.

他的毛衣放到热水里一洗就缩小了。- His sweater shrank when washed in hot water.

2046. 锁/suǒ/ - to lock; lock

2047. 谈判/tán pàn/ - to negotiate; negotiation

2048. 逃/táo/ - to escape; to flee

凶手最终还是逃了。- The killer finally escaped.

他逃进大山里。- He fled into the mountain.

2049. 逃避/táo bì/ - to evade; to avoid; to escape; to run away

她在试图逃避为自己的行为承担全部责任。- She is trying to evade all responsibility for her behavior.

据说有几百人为逃避逮捕而藏了起来。- Hundreds of people are said to have gone into hiding to avoid arrest.

狐狸正在试图逃避猎犬。- The fox is trying to escape from the hound.

你不能永远逃避。- You can't run away forever.

2050. 讨价还价/tǎo jià huán jià/ - to bargain

不要害怕讨价还价。- Don't be afraid to bargain.

2051. 疼爱/téng ài/ - to love dearly

2052. 提倡/tí chàng/ - to advocate

2053. 提问/tí wèn/ - to question

2054. 体会/tǐ huì/ - to get to know something (through learning or by experience)

2055. 体现/tǐ xiàn/ - to embody

2056. 体验/tǐ yàn/ - to experience (for oneself); experience

我需要从教育事业中抽出时间来体验人生。- I needed some time off from school to experience life.

这并不是我所期待的那种平静的体验。- It wasn't the peaceful experience I had expected.

2057. 调整/tiáo zhěng/ - to adjust; adjustment

2058. 挑战/tiǎo zhàn/ - to challenge; challenge

2059. 统一/tǒng yī/ - to unify

2060. 统治/tǒng zhì/ - to rule

2061. 偷/tōu/ - to steal

2062. 投资/tóu zī/ - to invest; investment

2063. 投入/tóu rù/ - to invest in; to put into; to throw into; to be absorbed

一大笔资金投入了各分公司。- A large amount of capital is invested in all these branches.

更经济地节能技术在发达国家已经投入使用。- More cost-effective energy conservation techniques have been put into operation in developed countries.

老实交税，不然的话就与可能被投入监狱。- Pay your taxes honestly, or you may be thrown into jail.

我做事太过投入以致于对周围发生的事毫无反应。- I got so absorbed in doing something that I was unaware of what happened around me.

2064. 吐/tǔ/ - to spit

/tù/ - throw up; to vomit

2065. 推辞/tuī cí/ - to decline (an appointment, invitation, position, etc.)

2066. 推广/tuī guǎng/ - to popularize

2067. 推荐/tuī jiàn/ - to recommend; recommendation

2068. 退/tuì/ - to move back

2069. 退步/tuì bù/ - to regress

2070. 退休/tuì xiū/ - to retire; retirement

2071. 完善/wán shàn/ - to perfect; to improve

他把更多时间用于完善舞蹈动作，而不是健身训练。- He spent more time perfecting his dance moves instead of doing gym work.

外科手术的技术不断得到完善。- Surgical techniques are constantly being improved.

2072. 往返/wǎng fǎn/ - to come and go; to go there and back

2073. 危害/wēi hài/ - to endanger

扩大城市面积危害野生动植物。- The spread of urban areas endangers wildlife.

2074. 威胁/wēi xié/ - to threaten; threat

2075. 违反/wéi fǎn/ - to violate

2076. 维护/wéi hù/ - to maintain; maintenance

2077. 围绕/wéi rào/ - to revolve around

整部电影围绕毒品、性和暴力来展开。- The entire film revolves around drugs, sex and, violence.

2078. 委屈/wěi qu/ - to feel wronged

2079. 委托/wěi tuō/ - to entrust

2080. 问候/wèn hòu/ - to greet

2081. 吸取/xī qǔ/ - to absorb; to draw

你想吸取你需要的知识就得付出时间和努力。- It takes time and effort for one to absorb the knowledge they need.

我们可以从大师们的作品中吸取营养。- We can draw nourishment from the masterpieces.

2082. 吸收/xī shōu/ - to absorb

干沙子易吸水。- Dry sand absorbs water easily.

2083. 下载/xià zǎi/ - to download

2084. 显得/xiǎn de/ - to seem; to look

他显得有点紧张。- He seems a bit nervous.

他显得苍老了。- He looks old.

2085. 显示/xiǎn shì/ – to show; to display

2086. 相处/xiāng chǔ/ – to get along

2087. 相关/xiāng guān/ – to be related to

2088. 想念/xiǎng niàn/ – to miss

2089. 想象/xiǎng xiàng/ – to imagine

2090. 享受/xiǎng shòu/ – to enjoy

2091. 象征/xiàng zhēng/ – to symbolize; to stand for; symbol

2092. 消费/xiāo fèi/ – to consume

2093. 消化/xiāo huà/ – to digest; digestion

2094. 消灭/xiāo miè/ – to annihilate; to eliminate

2095. 消失/xiāo shī/ – to disappear

2096. 销售/xiāo shòu/ – to sell; sale

2097. 歇/xiē/ – to take a rest

让我歇一下。– Please let me take a rest.

2098. 协调/xié tiáo/ – to cohere; to coordinate

装饰物与设计的基调不协调。– The decorations do not cohere with the basic design.

必须协调好城市规划和土地分配之间的关系。– City planning and land allocation has to be coordinated.

2099. 欣赏/xīn shǎng/ – to appreciate

任何人都能欣赏我们的音乐。– Anyone can appreciate our music.

2100. 形成/xíng chéng/ – to form

2101. 形容/xíng róng/ – to describe

2102. 醒/xǐng/ – to wake

2103. 修改/xiū gǎi/ – to amend; to modify

2104. 叙述/xù shù/ – to relate (a story or information)

2105. 宣布/xuān bù/ – to declare; to announce

2106. 宣传/xuān chuán/ – to disseminate

2107. 选举/xuǎn jǔ/ – to elect; election

2108. 询问/xún wèn/ - to inquire
2109. 寻找/xún zhǎo/ - to look for; to seek
2110. 训练/xùn liàn/ - to train; training
2111. 延长/yán cháng/ - to extend; to prolong
2112. 痒/yǎng/ - to itch; itchy
2113. 咬/yǎo/ - to bite
2114. 移动/yí dòng/ - to move; mobile
2115. 移民/yí mín/ - to immigrate; immigration
2116. 遗憾/yí hàn/ - to regret; regret, pity

我遗憾地接受了他的辞职。- I accepted his resignation with regret

我很遗憾地通知你他已因伤势太重不治身亡了。- I regret to inform you that he died as a result of his injuries.

真遗憾！- What a pity!

2117. 一路平安/yí lù píng ān/ - to have a pleasant journey
2118. 议论/yì lùn/ - to talk about

不要在背后议论别人。- Don't talk about others behind their backs.

2119. 印刷/yìn shuā/ - to print; printing
2120. 迎接/yíng jiē/ - to receive (someone)

他到车站迎接客人去了。- He went to the door to greet his visitors.

2121. 营业/yíng yè/ - to open (for business)

超市上午九点开始营业。- The supermarket opens at nine in the morning.

2122. 应付/yìng fu/ - to deal with; to cope with; to make do; perfunctory

我觉得我能应付。- I think I can deal with it.

他能够应付当前的形势。- He can cope with the present situation.

我这个提包还能应付一阵子。- I can make do with this handbag for some time.

对客户采取应付态度是不对的。- It would be wrong to adopt a perfunctory attitude towards clients.

/yīng fù/ - payable

我们下个月会付大额应付账款吗？- Shall we pay the majority of our accounts payable next month?

2123. 应聘/yìng pìn/ - to apply for a position

2124. 应用/yìng yòng/ - to use; to apply; application

这种药应用广泛。- This medicine is widely used.

他的想法是将几何学应用到力学上。- His idea was to apply geometry to dynamics.

我不用退出游戏就可以打开其他应用程序。- I can open other applications without having to exit my game.

拥抱/yōng bào/ - to hug; to embrace; to hold in one's arms; hug

2125. 油炸/yóu zhá/ - to fry

2126. 游览/yóu lǎn/ - to go sightseeing

2127. 犹豫/yóu yù/ - to hesitate

2128. 娱乐/yú lè/ - to amuse; amusement; entertainment

2129. 预订/yù dìng/ - to reserve; reservation

2130. 预防/yù fáng/ - to take precautions against

2131. 运输/yùn shū/ - to transport; transportation

2132. 运用/yùn yòng/ - to apply

这样他们就能更好地把理论运用到实践中去。- In this way, they can better apply theory to practice.

2133. 在乎/zài hu/ - to care about

2134. 赞成/zàn chéng/ - to approve; to agree with

2135. 赞美/zàn měi/ - to eulogize

2136. 造成/zào chéng/ - to cause

2137. 责备/zé bèi/ - to blame

2138. 摘/zhāi/ - to pick (flowers, fruit, etc.); to take off (glasses, hat, etc.)

2139. 粘贴/zhān tiē/ - to paste

2140. 展开/zhǎn kāi/ - to unfold

2141. 涨/zhǎng/ - to rise (of prices, rivers)

2142. 掌握/zhǎng wò/ - to master

2143. 招待/zhāo dài/ - to entertain

我再也不想招待客人了。- I don't want to entertain guests anymore.

2144. 着火/zháo huǒ/ - to catch fire

2145. 着凉/zháo liáng/ - to catch a cold

2146. 召开/zhào kāi/ - to convene (a conference or meeting)

2147. 针对/zhēn duì/ - to be directed against; to be aimed at

该条约不针对任何第三国。- The treaty is not directed against any third country.

这些话不是针对你说的。- These remarks are not aimed at you.

2148. 珍惜/zhēn xī/ - to cherish; to value; to treasure

2149. 诊断/zhěn duàn/ - to diagnose; diagnosis

2150. 振动/zhèn dòng/ - to vibrate; vibration

2151. 睁/zhēng/ - to open (eyes)

2152. 争论/zhēng lùn/ - to argue; to debate; argument

2153. 争取/zhēng qǔ/ - to fight for; to win over

2154. 征求/zhēng qiú/ - to solicit; to request (opinions, feedback, etc.)

2155. 挣钱/zhèng qián/ - to make money

2156. 执行/zhí xíng/ - to carry out; to implement

2157. 指导/zhǐ dǎo/ - to guide; guidance

2158. 指挥/zhǐ huī/ - to command; commander

2159. 制定/zhì dìng/ - to formulate; to draw up

2160. 制作/zhì zuò/ - to make

我用纸和胶水制作了一个模型。- I made a model out of paper and glue.

2161. 治疗/zhì liáo/ - to cure; medical treatment; cure

他的癌症只能控制，无法治疗。- His cancer can only be controlled, not cured.

她正在进行治疗。- She is under medical treatment.

尚没有治疗感冒的特效药。- There is still no cure for a cold.

2162. 煮/zhǔ/ - to boil

2163. 主持/zhǔ chí/ - to host

2164. 主动/zhǔ dòng/ - to take the initiative

2165. 嘱咐/zhǔ fu/ - to enjoin

2166. 祝福/zhù fú/ - to wish; blessings

你父亲和我都祝福你。- You father and I wish you well.

我们向您献上新年的祝福。- We offer new year blessings to you.

2167. 注册/zhù cè/ - to register (a company, website, etc.)

2168. 抓紧/zhuā jǐn/ - to grasp firmly; to hold on tight

2169. 专心/zhuān xīn/ - to concentrate; concentration

2170. 转变/zhuǎn biàn/ - to change

2171. 转告/zhuǎn gào/ - to pass on (news, messages, information, etc.)

2172. 装饰/zhuāng shì/ - to decorate; decoration

2173. 追求/zhuī qiú/ - to pursue

2174. 咨询/zī xún/ - to consult; consultation

2175. 自豪/zì háo/ - to be proud of someone or something (in a good way)

2176. 组成/zǔ chéng/ - to form; to compose

他们组成了一个中文初级班。- They formed a group for beginners in Chinese.

海水主要由水和盐组成。- Seawater is mainly composed of water and salt.

2177. 组合/zǔ hé/ - to assemble; combination

2178. 阻止/zǔ zhǐ/ - to prevent

2179. 醉/zuì/ - to be drunk

2180. 尊敬/zūn jìng/ - to respect

2181. 遵守/zūn shǒu/ - to comply with; to abide by

2182. 综合/zōng hé/ - to synthesize; comprehensive

你能把这些文件综合成一个吗？- Can you combine these files into one?

学生正在进行全学期功课的综合复习。- The students were doing a comprehensive review of the semester's work.

Chapter 10. Other Content and Function Words (A ~ L)

2183. 暧昧/ài mèi/ - ambiguous

   2184. 昂贵/áng guì/ - very expensive

   2185. 暗/àn/ - dark; gloomy

   2186. 霸道/bà dào/ - overbearing

   2187. 薄/báo/ - thin (of thickness)

   2188. 宝贵/bǎo guì/ - valuable; precious

   2189. 悲观/bēi guān/ - pessimistic

   2190. 必然/bì rán/ - inevitable

   2191. 必需/bì xū/ - necessary; essential

这些参考书是我们所必需的。- These reference books are necessary to us.

为了帮助提供必需得营养,我们调配了这些营养饮品。- To help provide essential nourishment, we've put together these nutritious drinks.

2192. 必要/bì yào/ - necessary; essential

所有必要条件都满足了。- All the necessary conditions were fulfilled.

我们有必要处理这个棘手的问题。- It is essential that we tackle this thorny problem.

2193. 博大精深/bó dà jīng shēn/ - broad and profound

2194. 不断/bú duàn/ - constant; continuous

2195. 不耐烦/bú nài fán/ - impatience; impatient; impatiently

她做了个不耐烦的动作。- She made a movement of impatience.

要知道我当时已经不耐烦了。- You know, I was getting impatient.

"我都说了我愿意,"他不耐烦地说。- "I told you I did," he replied impatiently.

2196. 不要紧/bú yào jǐn/ - unimportant; nothing serious; it doesn't matter; never mind

这鞋小点不要紧,穿穿就大了。- It doesn't matter if the shoes feel a bit tight, they'll stretch with wear.

不要紧。心意到了就行。- Never mind. It's the thought that counts.

这只是件不要紧的小事。- This is just an unimportant issue.

有点感冒,不要紧。- Just a slight cold, nothing serious

2197. 不像话/bú xiàng huà/ - unreasonable; outrageous

2198. 不安/bù ān/ - unpeaceful; worried; disturbed

听了这消息我心里很不安。- I was rather disturbed by the news.

2199. 不可思议/bù kě sī yì/ - inconceivable

2200. 不相上下/bú xiāng shàng xià/ - to be roughly the same; to be about equal

2201. 不足/bù zú/ - insufficient; not enough; inadequate

2202. 残酷/cán kù/ - cruel

2203. 惭愧/cán kuì/ - ashamed

2204. 残忍/cán rěn/ - ruthless

2205. 苍白/cāng bái/ - pale

2206. 超级/chāo jí/ - super

2207. 潮湿/cháo shī/ - moist; damp

2208. 彻底/chè dǐ/ - thorough; thoroughly

2209. 沉默/chén mò/ - silent

2210. 诚恳/chéng kěn/ - sincere

2211. 持续/chí xù/ - sustainable; to continue

2212. 迟疑/chí yí/ - hesitate

2213. 充分/chōng fèn/ - abundant

2214. 抽象/chōu xiàng/ - abstract

2215. 丑/chǒu/ - ugly

2216. 臭/chòu/ - stink; smelly

2217. 出色/chū sè/ - remarkable

2218. 初级/chū jí/ - primary

2219. 垂直/chuí zhí/ - vertical

2220. 次要/cì yào/ - secondary

2221. 匆忙/cōng máng/ - hasty

2222. 粗糙/cū cāo/ - rough (of surface, feeling, etc.)

2223. 大方/dà fang/ - generous

2224. 大型/dà xíng/ - largescale; wide scale; broadscale

2225. 单纯/dān chún/ - innocent; simple; merely

她很单纯。- She's innocent.

她像个孩子一样单纯。- She is as simple as a child.

在生产中不要单纯地追求数量。- Don't merely strive for quantity of production.

2226. 单调/dān diào/ - monotonous

2227. 单独/dān dú/ - by oneself; on one's own; alone

2228. 淡/dàn/ - light (in color); tasteless

2229. 当地/dāng dì/ - local; in the locality

2230. 地道/dì dao/ - pure; typical

她的上海话说得真地道。- She speaks in a pure Shanghai dialect.

他是个地道的美国人。- He is a typical American.

/dì dào/ - tunnel

2231. 独立/dú lì/ - independent; independence

2232. 独特/dú tè/ - unique; distinct

2233. 多余/duō yú/ - superfluous; unnecessary

这么做是多余的。- It is unnecessary to do this.

2234. 恶劣/è liè/ - vile; appalling

天气一直很恶劣。- The weather was consistently vile.

他们已经在恶劣的条件下生活了两个月了。- They have been living in the most appalling conditions for the last two months.

2235. 发达/fā dá/ - developed

2236. 繁荣/fán róng/ - prosperous; booming (economy)

2237. 疯狂/fēng kuáng/ - crazy; madness

2238. 干脆/gān cuì/ - straightforward; clear-cut

2239. 高档/gāo dàng/ - superior quality; top grade

2240. 个人/gè rén/ - individual

2241. 根本/gēn běn/ - fundamental; basic; basis

2242. 公开/gōng kāi/ - public; to make public

没有人对总统公开表示反对。- There's no public demonstration of opposition to the president.

他就队伍的表现公开道歉。- He made a public apology for the team's performance.

2243. 公平/gōng píng/ - fair

2244. 古典/gǔ diǎn/ - classical; classic

2245. 固定/gù dìng/ - static; to stabilize

2246. 乖/guāi/ - well behaved; (of a child or pet) obedient

2247. 光滑/guāng huá/ - smooth; sleek

2248. 光明/guāng míng/ - bright

2249. 广大/guǎng dà/ - vast

2250. 广泛/guǎng fàn/ - extensive; wide range

2251. 豪华/háo huá/ - luxurious

2252. 好客/hào kè/ - hospitality; to treat guests well; hospitable

2253. 好奇/hào qí/ - curious

2254. 合法/hé fǎ/ - lawful; legal

2255. 合理/hé lǐ/ - reasonable

2256. 怀孕/huái yùn/ - pregnant; pregnancy

2257. 慌张/huāng zhāng/ - panic; flurried

2258. 活跃/huó yuè/ - active; vigorous

2259. 基本/jī běn/ - basic; fundamental

2260. 激烈/jī liè/ - intense

2261. 寂寞/jì mò/ - lonely; alone

2262. 坚强/jiān qiáng/ - staunch; strong

她是个坚强而有原则的女人。- She is a strong, principled woman.

2263. 艰巨/jiān jù/ - arduous (task); formidable (project)

任务艰巨，同时时间又很紧迫。- The task is arduous, and there's also not much time.

该工程非常艰巨。- This is a formidable project.

2264. 坚决/jiān jué/ - firmly; resolutely; determined

我坚决不向病毒屈服。- I was determined not to succumb to the virus.

2265. 艰苦/jiān kǔ/ - difficult (of circumstances); hard (of time); arduous (of work); awful (of condition)

艰苦的环境能磨炼人的意志。- Difficult circumstances can temper one's will.

对她而言，那是一段非常艰苦的岁月。- It had been a hard time for her.

我们要耐着性子做艰苦的工作。- We must have patience in doing arduous work.

那里的条件很艰苦。- The conditions there are awful.

2266. 尖锐/jiān ruì/ - keen; sharp; bitter (of criticism)

他看问题很尖锐。- He sees things with a keen eye.

这些话讲得尖锐，但值得考虑。- These remarks are quite sharp, but worth consideration.

他对政府提出了尖锐的批评。- He levied bitter criticism against the government.

2267. 狡猾/jiǎo huá/ - crafty

2268. 结实/jiē shi/ - solid; sturdy; sturdily

这把椅子很结实。- This is a very solid chair.

这孩子又结实又健康。- This child is sturdy and healthy.

这艘船造得结实。- This boat was sturdily made.

2269. 紧/jǐn/ - tight

2270. 紧急/jǐn jí/ - urgent; emergency

2271. 谨慎/jǐn shèn/ - cautious

2272. 经典/jīng diǎn/ - classical; the classics

2273. 敬爱/jìng ài/ - respected

2274. 具体/jù tǐ/ - concrete; specific

2275. 巨大/jù dà/ - gigantic; enormous

2276. 均匀/jūn yún/ - well distributed; uniform

2277. 可见/kě jiàn/ - it can clearly be seen; visible

2278. 可靠/kě kào/ - reliable

2279. 可怕/kě pà/ - fearful; awful; frightful; to be afraid of; terrifying

我刚做了个非常可怕的梦。- I just had the most awful dream.

没有什么可怕的。- There's nothing to be afraid of.

昨晚他再次体验到了那种可怕的折磨。- Last night, he relived his terrifying ordeal.

2280. 客观/kè guān/ - objective

我很想听听你对此事的客观见解。- I would really like to have your objective opinion on this.

2281. 恐怖/kǒng bù/ - horrible; terror

2282. 空闲/kòng xián/ - free (time); idle

2283. 宽/kuān/ - wide; broad; width

2284. 老实/lǎo shi/ - frank

老实跟你讲，我可能犯了个错。- To be frank with you, I may have made a mistake.

2285. 乐观/lè guān/ - optimistic

2286. 立方/lì fāng/ - cubic

2287. 连忙/lián máng/ - promptly

2288. 连续/lián xù/ - continuous

2289. 良好/liáng hǎo/ - good

2290. 了不起/liǎo bu qǐ/ - amazing; great

我最喜欢的书是《了不起的盖茨比》。- *The Great Gatsby* is my favorite book.

2291. 灵活/líng huó/ - flexible

2292. 密切/mì qiè/ - to be close with; closely; intimate

我和她关系密切。- I'm close with her.

轻工业和农业密切相关。- Light industry is closely related to agriculture.

在中世纪，宗教和炼金术密切相联。- Religion had an intimate association with alchemy during the Middle Ages.

2293. 苗条/miáo tiáo/ - slim

2294. 明显/míng xiǎn/ - obvious; distinct

2295. 模糊/mó hu/ - vague; obscure; to blur

我对这意义还很模糊。- The meaning is still obscure to me.

我对第一见面的记忆很模糊。- My memory of that first meeting was vague.

汗水从额头流到了眼睛里，模糊了他的视线。- Sweat ran from his forehead into his eyes, blurring his vision.

2296. 陌生/mò shēng/ - unfamiliar

2297. 难看/nán kàn/ - ugly

2298. 难免/nán miǎn/ - hard to avoid; difficult to escape from

2299. 能干/néng gàn/ - competent

2300. 疲劳/pí láo/ - tired

2301. 片面/piàn miàn/ - unilateral

2302. 平常/píng cháng/ - ordinary; common; usually

2303. 平等/píng děng/ - equal; equality

2304. 平方/píng fāng/ - square (as in square meter)

2305. 平静/píng jìng/ - calm; tranquil

2306. 迫切/pò qiè/ - urgent

2307. 平均/píng jūn/ - on average; average

2308. 朴素/pǔ sù/ - simple

她穿了身朴素的浅灰色套装。- She was wearing a simple light gray suit.

2309. 谦虚/qiān xū/ - modest

2310. 浅/qiǎn/ - shallow; light (of color)

2311. 巧妙/qiǎo miào/ - ingenious

2312. 亲爱/qīn ài/ - dear

2313. 亲切/qīn qiè/ - lovely; friendly

2314. 勤劳/qín láo/ - industrious; hardworking

他是一个勤劳的人。- He is an industrious man.

中国人民勤劳而勇敢。- Chinese people are brave and hardworking.

2315. 清淡/qīng dàn/ - light (of food, not greasy or strongly favored)

2316. 全面/quán miàn/ - comprehensive

2317. 热烈/rè liè/ - warm (welcome, applause, etc.)

2318. 热心/rè xīn/ - enthusiastic; warmhearted

2319. 日常/rì cháng/ - daily

2320. 荣幸/róng xìng/ - honor; to be honored

今天很荣幸能参加你们的晚会。- It is a great honor to be with you at this evening party.

承蒙热情接待，不胜荣幸。- I am greatly honored to be given such a warm reception.

2321. 弱/ruò/ - weak

2322. 傻/shǎ/ - silly; foolish

2323. 善良/shàn liáng/ - kindhearted

2324. 深刻/shēn kè/ - profound

2325. 神秘/shén mì/ - mysterious

2326. 生动/shēng dòng/ - vivid; lively

2327. 时髦/shí máo/ - fashionable; fashion

她穿着一件时髦的裙装。- She wears a fashionable dress.

为赶时髦她花了不少钱。- She spent a lot of money to follow fashion trends.

2328. 时尚/shí shàng/ - fashionable; fashion

在阳光充足的地方过冬成了富人的时尚。- It became fashionable for the rich to spend winter in sunny areas.

《时尚》是美国很受欢迎的杂志。- *Fashion* is a very popular magazine in America.

2329. 实用/shí yòng/ - practical

2330. 手工/shǒu gōng/ - handmade; manual

2331. 舒适/shū shì/ - cozy; comfortable

2332. 熟练/shú liàn/ - skilled
我能够熟练操作电脑。- I'm skilled in operating a computer.

2333. 数码/shù mǎ/ - digital

2334. 私人/sī rén/ - private

2335. 所谓/suǒ wèi/ - so-called

2336. 坦率/tǎn shuài/ - frankness; frank; frankly
她似乎不够坦率。- She seemed to be lacking in frankness.
你可以跟我坦率一点。- You can be frank with me.
坦率来说，我不知道。- Frankly, I don't know why.

2337. 淘气/táo qì/ - naughty

2338. 特殊/tè shū/ - special

2339. 特意/tèyì/ - specially

2340. 体贴/tǐ tiē/ - considerate

2341. 天真/tiān zhēn/ - naïve; innocent

2342. 调皮/tiáo pí/ - naughty

2343. 通常/tōng cháng/ - usual; usually

2344. 痛苦/tòng kǔ/ - suffering; painful

2345. 透明/tòu míng/ - transparent

2346. 完美/wán měi/ - perfect; perfectly; perfection

2347. 完整/wán zhěng/ - complete
这是个完整的故事吗？- Is this a complete story?

2348. 唯一/wéi yī/ - only
这是我能够想到的唯一理由。- This is the only explanation I can think of.

2349. 伟大/wěi dà/ - great
他是个伟大的音乐家。- He is a great musician.

2350. 温暖/wēn nuǎn/ - warm

2351. 温柔/wēn róu/ - tender; gentle

2352. 文明/wén míng/ - civilized; civilization

2353. 稳定/wěn dìng/ - steady; stable; stability; to stabilize

2354. 无奈/wú nài/ - have no choice

万般无奈，我只好自己想办法。- I had no choice but to think of a way out by myself.

2355. 无数/wú shù/ - countless

2356. 无所谓/wú suǒ wèi/ - cannot be said to be; not to matter

这些发明无所谓什么实用价值。- These inventions can't be said to have much practical value.

你是输是赢都无所谓。- It doesn't matter if you win or lose.

2357. 无耻/wú chǐ/ - shameless

2358. 无畏/wú wèi/ - fearless

2359. 瞎/xiā/ - blind

2360. 鲜艳/xiān yàn/ - bright-colored

2361. 显然/xiǎn rán/ - obvious; obviously

2362. 相似/xiāng sì/ - similar; alike

我和他的看法相似。- My ideas are similar to his.

他们的性格很相似。- They are much alike in character.

2363. 消极/xiāo jí/ - negative

每个人都有积极和消极的时候。- Everyone has good and bad moments.

2364. 小气/xiǎo qi/ - petty

2365. 孝顺/xiào shùn/ - filial

她很孝顺父母。- She is extremely filial towards her parents.

2366. 形象/xíng xiàng/ - vivid; image

这树立起了一种强有力的公司形象。- This established a strong corporate image.

他用几句形象的话简述了局势。- He sketched the situation in a few vivid words.

2367. 幸运/xìng yùn/ - lucky; fortunate

你真是个幸运儿。- You are a lucky dog.

2368. 雄伟/xióng wěi/ - magnificent (of building, maintain, etc.)

2369. 虚心/xū xīn/ - modest
2370. 迅速/xùn sù/ - rapid
2371. 严肃/yán sù/ - solemn; solemnity
2372. 业余/yè yú/ - amateur
2373. 英俊/yīng jùn/ - handsome
2374. 拥挤/yōng jǐ/ - to be crowded; congestion
2375. 用功/yòng gōng/ - industrious (in one's studies)
她最近十分用工。- She is very industrious lately.
2376. 优惠/yōu huì/ - preferential
中国的投资政策为外国投资者提供了优惠待遇。- China's investment policy provides preferential treatment to foreign investors.
2377. 优美/yōu měi/ - graceful; beautiful
2378. 悠久/yōu jiǔ/ - long (about culture, tradition, history)
2379. 有利/yǒu lì/ - favorable
这些条款对他们公司有利。- These terms were favorable to their company.
2380. 糟糕/zāo gāo/ - terrible; awful
2381. 窄/zhǎi/ - narrow (of space, mind)
2382. 占线/zhàn xiàn/ - busy (phone calling)
2383. 整个/zhěng gè/ - whole; entire
我走遍了整个半岛。- I had walked around the entire peninsula.
整个程序又开始运行了。- The whole process started all over again.
2384. 重/zhòng/ - heavy (of weight)
2385. 重大/zhòng dà/ - significant
2386. 周到/zhōu dào/ - thoughtful; considerate
2387. 主观/zhǔ guān/ - subjective
2388. 紫/zǐ/ - purple

2389. 自动/zì dòng/ - automatic

2390. 自觉/zì jué/ - on one's own initiative

他学习很自觉。 - He studies on his own initiative.

2391. 自私/zì sī/ - selfish; selfishness

2392. 自愿/zì yuàn/ - of one's own will; voluntary

他辞去校长一职并非出于自愿。 - He did not resign as headmaster of his own volition.

定于下个月开始施行的方案是自愿性质的。 - The scheme, due to begin next month, will be voluntary.

2393. 自以为是/zì yǐ wéi shì/ - to be opinionated; to be self-righteous

2394 真实/zhēn shí/ - real

2395. 彼此/bǐ cǐ/ - each other

2396. 对方/duì fāng/ - the other side

2397. 个别/gè bié/ - just one or two

2398. 其余/qí yú/ - the rest; remaining

2399. 双方/shuāng fāng/ - both parties; both sides

2400. 他们/tā men/ - they (a group of males or mixed genders)

2401. 她们/tā men/ - they (a group of females)

2402. 它们/tā men/ - they (a group of things, animals, plants, etc.)

2403. 册/cè/ - measure word for books

2404. 吨/dūn/ - ton

2405. 幅/fú/ - measure word for paintings

2406. 届/jiè/ - measure word for events, meetings, elections, sporting fixtures, etc.

2407. 颗/kē/ - measure word for small spheres, pearls, corn grains, teeth, satellites, etc

2408. 克/kè/ - gram

2409. 厘米/lí mǐ/ - centimeter

2410. 秒/miǎo/ - second (time unity); in a very short time

2411. 匹/pǐ/ - measure word for horses, cloth, etc.

2412. 片/piàn/ - measure word for slices, tablets, tracts of land or areas of water, etc.

2413. 项/xiàng/ - measure word for principles, items, clauses, etc.; surname Xiang

2414. 毕竟/bì jìng/ - after all; all in all

2415. 不见得/bú jiàn de/ - not necessarily; not likely
他今晚不见得回来。- He's not likely to come tonight.
对于这种事，发火不见得是最有用的或最能被接受的反应。- Anger is not necessarily the most useful or acceptable reaction to such events.

2416. 不得了/bù dé liǎo/ - desperately serious; extremely; terribly
没什么不得了的事。- There's nothing desperately serious.
她听到那坏消息后伤心得不得了。- She was terribly sad when she heard the bad news.
生意好的不得了。- Business is extremely good.

2417. 曾经/céng jīng/ - previously; ever

2418. 迟早/chí zǎo/ - sooner or later

2419. 从前/cóng qián/ - previously; once upon a time

2420. 的确/dí què/ - indeed

2421. 纷纷/fēn fēn/ - one after another; one by one

2422. 赶快/gǎn kuài/ - immediately; at once

2423. 格外/gé wài/ - especially; particularly

2424. 各自/gè zì/ - respectively

2425. 果然/guǒ rán/ - sure enough; as expected

2426. 过分/guò fèn/ - excessively; excessive

2427. 忽然/hū rán/ - suddenly; all of a sudden

2428. 急忙/jí máng/ - hastily

2429. 简直/jiǎn zhí/ - simply; at all

他的中文简直糟透了。- His Chinese is simply terrible.

这玩意儿简直一点用都没有。- This thing is completely useless.

2430. 尽量/jìn liàng/ - as much as possible; to the greatest extent

2431. 绝对/jué duì/ - absolutely; absolute

2432. 居然/jū rán/ - to one's surprise; unexpectedly

2433. 立即/lì jí/ - immediately

我军立即进行了反击。- Our troops immediately returned fire.

立刻/lì kè/ - at once; immediately

立刻到这来！- Come here at once.

我们会立刻送一份报价给你。- We'll send you a quote immediately.

2434. 临时/lín shí/ - temporarily; temporary

2435. 陆续/lù xù/ - successively; one after another

2436. 目前/mù qián/ - currently; at the present time

2437. 偶然/ǒu rán/ - incidentally; occasional; by chance

2438. 强烈/qiáng liè/ - violently

2439. 悄悄/qiāo qiāo/ - stealthily

2440. 亲自/qīn zì/ - personally

2441. 轻易/qīng yì/ - easily; readily

我不轻易交朋友。- I don't readily make friends.

如果你以为你能轻易打败他，那你会后悔的。- If you think you can easily defeat him, you will regret it.

2442. 忍不住/rěn bu zhù/ - cannot help

2443. 如今/rú jīn/ - nowadays

2444. 始终/shǐ zhōng/ - from beginning to end

2445. 事先/shì xiān/ - in advance

2446. 说不定/shuō bu dìng/ - can't say for sure; may

他说不定走了。- He may have left.

我也说不定。- I can't say for sure.

2447. 丝毫/sī háo/ - at all

这丝毫不会影响我的判断。- It doesn't affect my judgment at all.

2448. 随时/suí shí/ - at any time

2449. 同时/tóng shí/ - at the same time; simultaneously

2450. 相当/xiāng dāng/ - equivalent to

2451. 相对/xiāng duì/ - relatively; face to face

湿度相对较低。- The humidity is relatively low.

我们俩相对而坐。- We were sitting face to face.

2452. 幸亏/xìng kuī/ - fortunately; luckily

幸亏在我们动身前雨就停了。- Fortunately, the rain stopped before we set off.

2453. 依然/yī rán/ - as before; still

2454. 再三/zài sān/ - over and over again

2455. 照常/zhào cháng/ - as usual

2456. 逐步/zhú bù/ - step by step

2457. 逐渐/zhú jiàn/ - gradually

2458. 总算/zǒng suàn/ - at last; finally

你总算回来了！- You're finally back!

开了三天车，总算到家了。- After driving for three days, we finally got home.

2459. 最初/zuì chū/ - at the very beginning

2460. 不然/bù rán/ - or else

2461. 不如/bù rú/ - not as good as; it would be better to

2462. 除非/chú fēi/ - only if; unless

2463. 此外/cǐ wài/ - besides; in addition; furthermore

2464. 从此/cóng cǐ/ - from now on; since then

2465. 从而/cóng ér/ - thus; thereby

2466. 多亏/duō kuī/ - thanks to

2467. 反而/fǎn ér/ - instead; on the contrary

2468. 反复/fǎn fù/ - repeatedly; over and over

2469. 反正/fǎn zhèng/ - whatever happens; anyway

2470. 仿佛/fǎng fú/ - as if

2471. 怪不得/guài bu de/ - no wonder

2472. 何必/hé bì/ - there is no need

2473. 何况/hé kuàng/ - much less; let alone

2474. 或许/huò xǔ/ - perhaps; maybe

2475. 假如/jiǎ rú/ - supposing; if

2476. 据说/jù shuō/ - it is said that

2477. 看来/kàn lái/ - it seems; it appears; looks likely

2478. 宁可/nìng kě/ - would rather

2479. 是否/shì fǒu/ - whether (or not)

2480. 似的/shì de/ - as if

他们完全忽略了这些事实，就仿佛不存在似的。- They completely ignore these facts as if they never existed.

2481. 似乎/sì hū/ - to seem; as if

前途似乎不太乐观。- The future doesn't seem very hopeful.

听起来他们似乎犯下了一个可怕的错误。- It sounds as if they might have made a terrible mistake.

2482. 万一/wàn yī/ - just in case; what if

为防万一，我还给他买了一份保险。- I bought an insurance for him just in case.

万一你错了呢？- What if you are wrong?

2483. 要不/yào bu/ - how about

要不我们去吃中餐？- How about having Chinese food?

2484. 一旦/yí dàn/ - in case (something happens)

2485. 一再/yí zài/ - again and again

2486. 以及/yǐ jí/ - as well as

2487. 以来/yǐ lái/ - since

该党自 1964 年独立以来一直执政。- The party has been in power since the country's independence in 1964.

2488. 与其/yǔ qí/ - rather than

与其坐以待毙不如主动出击。- It's better to take the initiative rather than to wait for death.

2489. 至今/zhì jīn/ - until now

2490. 至于/zhì yú/ - as for

2491. 自从/zì cóng/ - since

自从去年至今他都没回过家。- He hasn't been home since last year.

2492. 总共/zǒng gòng/ - altogether; in total

2493. 总之/zǒng zhī/ - in a word

2494. 作为/zuò wéi/ - as; conduct

作为作家，我对人物塑造感兴趣。- As a writer, I am interested in characterization.

他的作为无可厚非。- His conduct was blameless.

2495. 啊/a/ - modal particle ending sentence, showing affirmation, approval, exclamation, query, or consent; ah

2496. 哎/āi/ - hey! (interjection used to attract attention or to express surprise or disapprobation)

哎！你听见没有？- Hey! Are you listening to me?

你很讨厌哎！- You're annoying!

2497. 唉/āi/ - to sigh; (interjection to express agreement or recognition)

2498. 哎哟/āi yō/ - ouch

2499. 唉/āi/ - to sigh; (interjection to express agreement or recognition)

2500. 吧/ba/ - (modal particle indicating polite suggestion)

我们去公园吧。- Why don't we go to the park?

Conclusion

Congratulations on making it through to the end. This book should have been useful and informative and provided you with a sound grasp of basic Chinese words.

To wrap up, here are some tips and recommendations for further study:

1. Don't learn just ONE word; learn the WHOLE sentence.

Have you noticed that sometimes when you learn just a single word, you can recognize it and even explain the meaning, but you have no clue how to use it? To avoid this situation, you should watch the context and how you can use this word. Although this book has provided some examples for some hard words, you still need to gather as many example sentences as you can. Yes, it will take more time, but the results should be immediately obvious!

2. To remember a new word, just use it.

Sound easy? - It is!

The hardest part is not to forget about using one new word per day.

Set a goal - to learn one new word every day. You can choose a word in the morning or evening, look at how to use it, then find some examples and the context. You can also prepare some phrases which you can use during the day in advance. Then just go out and use it! Use it at least three times, and then you'll definitely be able to remember it. You also can try to use the same phrase with different people. The most important thing is just to use it as much as you can.

3. Use memory cards.

One of the easiest ways to learn vocabulary that everyone knows, but often forgets, is memory cards. Instead of wasting time in a queue, you can do something useful, such as repeating words. They're very light so you can bring them everywhere. You will never know when you'll have some free time to repeat vocabulary.

4. Learn vocabulary from a specific topic.

For example, you choose the topic of cooking. Write out and learn all the nouns, verbs, adjectives, and phrases that are associated with cooking. After this, open any video, TV drama, or cartoon about cooking. Just listen to it and try to catch the words you've just learned. Hearing a newly learned word will surely make you remember it for a long time.

5. Incorporate surrounding things in your studies.

How many times a day do you look in the mirror? Now imagine that you stuck a sticker with the name of "mirror" in Chinese on it. You'll see this word so often that there is no way not to remember it. Again, it's better to write a simple sentence instead of just a single word.

Finally, it is recommended that you now take the time to review everything in this book again from the beginning. See if you can understand all the sections better the second time around.

Good luck with your language learning journey!

Manufactured by Amazon.ca
Bolton, ON